ANGER LANGUAGES

Understanding Why We React the Way We Do
& How to Break the Cycle

CYNTHIA A. DODGE, PH.D.

This is a work of nonfiction. To protect confidentiality, the names and identifying details in the case histories and vignettes referenced within this book have been changed. Any resemblance to persons living or dead is purely coincidental.

DEDICATION

This book is dedicated to the multiple mother figures in my life, who guided, supported, and nourished me early on, and throughout life—never in anger, but always with love—and to my daughter, who can continue the pattern.

AUTHOR'S NOTE

To protect confidentiality, the names and identifying details in the case histories and vignettes referenced within this book have been changed. Any resemblance to persons living or dead is purely coincidental.

TABLE OF CONTENTS

INTRODUCTION

The world is loud. Not simply busy, but saturated—filled with a constant barrage of images, opinions, outrage, and urgency. We move through our days surrounded by noise designed to capture attention, provoke reaction, and signal relevance. In such an environment, stillness feels increasingly rare, and reflection increasingly difficult. Amid this constant stimulation, many people feel destabilized. The effort required to sift through misinformation, performance, and competing narratives can leave us disoriented and fatigued.

Anger shows up in many forms—overt and explosive, quiet and corrosive, public and private. It is amplified through culture and carried silently in bodies. For some, it becomes a way to feel powerful or certain. For others, it turns inward, managing anxiety, tracking symptoms, or searching for guidance on how to function in an increasingly complex world. While these responses differ, neither is immune to the quiet toll of anger. In all its forms, anger reflects distress that has not yet found another way to be understood.

This book was written with the hope that suffering with or along side anger ;—and suffering from its effects—can be softened. The ideas presented here are an outgrowth of The Anger Addict, first published in 1991, of which I was a co-author with John R. Langevin, Ph.D. The lives portrayed in that book, and revisited here, are timeless. What has changed is our understanding of what those individuals were navigating—developmentally, relationally, and neurologically.

Advances in trauma-informed care, somatic healing, and relational neuroscience have expanded how we understand anger—not as a flaw to be eradicated, but as a pattern shaped by experience and reinforced over time. These insights have given rise to this new work, which seeks to translate anger from something to be feared or controlled into something that can be understood, regulated, and ultimately integrated.

In a world that favors reaction over reflection and performance over presence, this book offers an invitation: to slow down, to elevate understanding, and to rediscover the possibility of change through awareness, relationship, and connection.

The Anger Language Map

Anger does not appear in only one form.It is generally considered to be a single emotional state—something that must either be controlled, expressed, or eliminated. But in lived experience anger behaves more like a **language system**. It communicates distress, organizes power, and shapes relationships in distinct ways.

Just as spoken languages use different structures to convey meaning, so does anger. The emotion may look similar on the surface—raised voices, hurt feelings, tension—but the **function of the anger** can be very different.

Some anger pushes outward in confrontation.

Some anger turns inward and disappears into self-blame.

Some anger exerts pressure through emotional suffering.

Over time these patterns become familiar. Individuals begin to rely on them without necessarily recognizing that they are doing so. What feels like "just the way I react" is often a learned emotional language that developed in response to earlier experiences of vulnerability, power, or connection. This book explores six of the most common anger languages.

Behind the Smile—Passive Anger

Passive anger hides beneath politeness, compliance, or emotional restraint.

The individual may appear calm or agreeable on the surface while internally experiencing resentment, disappointment, or frustration. Direct confrontation feels uncomfortable or risky, so anger is managed through withdrawal, subtle resistance, or quiet disengagement.

Relationships affected by passive anger often feel confusing. The absence of open conflict can create the illusion that everything is fine, even as emotional distance quietly grows.

The Short Fuse—Explosive Anger

Explosive anger erupts quickly and intensely.In this pattern emotional activation rises rapidly and spills into outbursts of shouting, accusation, or dramatic reaction. The individual may feel overwhelmed by the speed and force of their own responses, sometimes regretting them soon afterward. The short fuse often develops in nervous systems that have learned to react quickly to perceived threat. What others experience as disproportionate intensity may feel, internally, like urgent self-protection.

You'll Get Yours—Retaliatory Anger

Retaliatory anger organizes itself around justice and retribution.

When someone feels wronged, insulted, or treated unfairly, the impulse is to restore balance by striking back—through criticism, confrontation, or punishment. The anger feels justified and purposeful.Although retaliatory anger can expose genuine injustice, it often traps individuals in escalating cycles of attack and defense where both parties become increasingly entrenched.

You're Killing Your Father—Guilt-Inducing Anger

In this language anger does not appear primarily as confrontation. Instead it travels through emotional suffering. Distress becomes the message. Pain signals that someone else has done something wrong. Others feel compelled to repair the distress even when the anger behind it has not been spoken directly.Over time relationships may begin to organize around emotional pressure rather than open negotiation, as others try to prevent the next episode of suffering.

You're Probably Right—Guilt-Absorbing Anger

Some individuals manage conflict by turning anger inward.

Rather than expressing frustration or disagreement, they assume responsibility for the distress around them. Apologies come quickly. Disagreements soften into accommodation. This strategy can preserve harmony in the short term, but over time resentment often accumulates quietly beneath the surface. The individual may begin to feel unseen, depleted, or emotionally trapped.

What Are You Looking At—Life-Stance Anger

For some people anger becomes less a reaction and more a stance toward the world.Life-stance anger is characterized by chronic vigilance, defensiveness, and a readiness to interpret situations as disrespectful or threatening. The individual moves through life prepared for confrontation.This posture often develops in environments where trust felt unsafe or vulnerability invited harm. Anger becomes a protective shield against anticipated injury.

Why Recognizing Anger Languages Matters

Most conflicts are not simply disagreements about events or decisions.

They are collisions between **different anger languages**.

One person explodes.

Another withdraws.

One expresses suffering to secure reassurance.

Another absorbs blame to keep the peace.

Each person believes they are responding reasonably. Yet the interaction becomes confusing because each participant is interpreting the other's behavior through a different emotional language. Learning to recognize these patterns changes how anger is understood. Instead of asking *"Why are you so angry?"* a more useful question becomes:

"What language of anger is being spoken here?" When the language becomes visible, new options appear. Individuals can begin translating what anger is trying to communicate and develop more direct ways of expressing the needs beneath it.

Anger does not disappear. But its message becomes easier to understand.

And when anger can be understood, it no longer has to dominate the conversation.

Six Ways Anger Communicates Distress

Behind the Smile—Passive Anger

When direct protest feels unsafe, anger hides behind politeness, distance, or quiet resistance.

The Short Fuse—Explosive Anger

When emotional pressure rises too quickly to contain, anger erupts in sudden bursts of intensity.

You'll Get Yours—Retaliatory Anger

When someone feels wronged, anger seeks to restore balance by striking back.

You're Killing Your Father—Guilt-Inducing Anger

When anger cannot be expressed directly, suffering becomes the message that pressures others to repair the harm.

You're Probably Right—Guilt-Absorbing Anger

When preserving connection feels more important than protest, anger turns inward and becomes self-blame.

What Are You Looking At—Life-Stance Anger

When the world feels fundamentally threatening, anger becomes a constant posture of vigilance and defense.

Anger does not speak in only one voice. It moves outward, inward, and between people, taking on recognizable patterns that shape our relationships and our sense of self.

The following map illustrates the different "languages" anger can speak.

The Anger Language Map

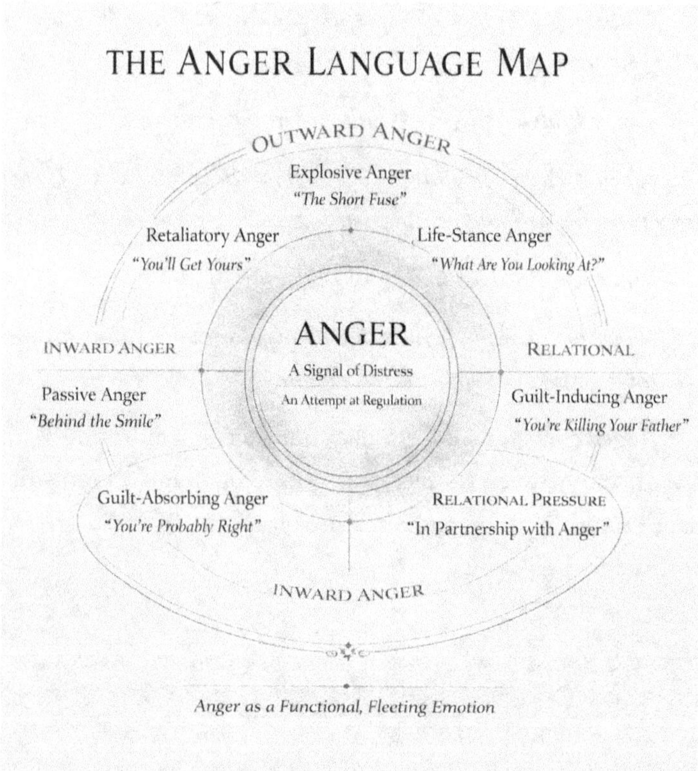

CHAPTER ONE

THE ARCHITECTURE OF ANGER

Introduction

We live in a noisy world. Outrage travels faster than understanding, reaction often replaces reflection, and emotional intensity is amplified rather than contained. Many people experience the world as angrier than it once was. Whether this perception reflects reality or visibility, it shapes how we interpret one another's behavior. Anger feels everywhere—in public discourse, in families, in workplaces, and often within ourselves.

Consider a familiar moment.

A couple stands in the kitchen late in the evening. One partner asks a simple question about something that didn't get done that day. The other hears accusation rather than curiosity. Within seconds voices rise, shoulders tense, and a conversation about an unfinished errand turns into an argument about respect, effort, and who carries the burden of the relationship.

Ten minutes later both are bewildered. Neither intended to start a fight. Both feel misunderstood. Each is certain the other "overreacted."

Moments like this make anger seem mysterious, irrational, or explosive. But anger is rarely random. It is structured.

There was a time when ordinary things were allowed to be quiet. Fruit, for example, once belonged to still life—objects observed, not performed. Apples and bananas were painted because they were simple, familiar, and unremarkable. Today, even fruit is rarely still. It is photographed, captioned, filtered, and posted, enlisted to amplify an experience or signal relevance. What was once observed is now performed.

This shift reflects a broader cultural pattern. Experience itself has become something to display rather than inhabit. In a world that rewards visibility and reaction, internal states are often externalized before they are understood. Anger, in this context, is not only expressed more loudly—it is invited, rewarded, and reinforced.

Most people experience anger not as a single emotion that simply appears and disappears, but as part of a recognizable pattern.

Anger follows recognizable pathways shaped by temperament, early relationships, learned expectations, and repeated experience. Over time these pathways become efficient, automatic, and predictable. Throughout this book they are referred to as Anger Languages – habitual ways individuals translate emotional distress into behavior. What appears to be spontaneous anger is often the activation of a well-established system.

Anger is often compared to an explosion, a storm, or a fire. However, anger is not just these dramatic forms. Continuing the metaphor of fruit, anger is also like a ripened orange on a tree.

When fruit appears, we see the result—bright, visible, undeniable. What we do not see are the roots underground, the seasons of growth, the invisible seeds inside that made the fruit possible.

An outburst, a withdrawal, a cutting remark, a depressive collapse—these are the visible outcomes of processes that have been developing quietly over time, much like the progression from orange blossom to ripened fruit. By the time anger appears, the conditions that produced it are already well established.

Focusing only on the ripened fruit, or in this case the angry expression, leads to misunderstanding. People attempt to remove the visible expression without addressing what sustains it. They apologize, suppress, promise to change, or blame circumstances—yet the pattern persists.

To understand anger, we must look beneath the surface. Anger at times makes no sense – UNTIL it does.

Anger is not merely something people do. It is something they have learned to rely on.

Just as people learn different languages to communicate, they also learn different languages of anger—distinct ways of expressing distress, protecting themselves, and managing vulnerability.

This book will offer a framework for understanding how anger functions, what it protects, and why it becomes so difficult to change when it has become a primary method of regulation.

Over many years of clinical work, I began to notice that anger rarely appeared randomly. Instead, it followed recognizable emotional pathways. Although each person's history is unique, certain patterns appeared again and again.

Across this book, five primary anger patterns will be explored:

Explosive Anger – anger that erupts suddenly and intensely

Passive Anger – anger expressed indirectly through withdrawal, delay, or compliance

Retaliatory Anger – anger that waits, remembers, and restores balance through revenge or punishment

Guilt-inducing anger- anger that binds others through responsibility for emotional suffering

Guilt-absorbing anger – anger turned inward as self-blame or excessive responsibility

Life stance anger – anger that becomes a worldview, shaping how the world itself is interpreted

Most books about anger focus on control: how to calm down, count to ten, vent safely, or avoid saying something regrettable. These strategies can be useful in the moment, but they rarely explain why the same conflicts return again and again. This book takes a different approach. Rather than treating anger simply as a problem to eliminate, it examines the underlying patterns through which anger operates. Each chapter explores one of these patterns—what it protects, how it develops, and why it becomes so difficult to change. When anger is understood as part of a larger system rather than a single emotion to be controlled, its logic becomes visible and new responses become possible.

These patterns are not personality types. They are adaptive systems, learned strategies—ways individuals learned to regulate distress, maintain connection, preserve control, or protect themselves from vulnerability.

Although these anger patterns appear very different, they share a common purpose. Each represents a strategy for protecting the individual from a form of vulnerability that once felt intolerable—shame, rejection, helplessness, or loss of control.

When anger is understood in this way, the question changes. Instead of asking how to eliminate anger, we begin asking what it has been protecting.

Anger can make sense when its origins are understood. Understanding these patterns allows anger to become intelligible rather than mysterious, purposeful rather than random.

The Anger Pathways

Anger tends to follow familiar pathways. Over time, individuals learn a pattern that feels reliable under stress. These patterns may include:

- Explosive escalation, followed by remorse
- Withdrawal, silence, or delayed retaliation
- Passive resistance, chronic "forgetting," or indirect sabotage

- Moralized anger organized around fairness, obligation, or righteousness
- Anger expressed through guilt—inducing it in others or absorbing it internally
- Anger turned inward as shame, depression, self-attack, or numbness

These are not moral categories. They are patterns of regulation.

Anger becomes problematic not because it exists, but because it becomes the only language available under stress.

Anger as Signal, Anger as Strategy

At its core, anger is a signal—an internal alert that something feels wrong, unfair, threatening, or out of alignment. In its healthiest form, it mobilizes attention and action toward self-protection, boundary-setting, or repair. But for many individuals, anger becomes more than a signal. It becomes a strategy.

When anger becomes the most accessible strategy for dealing with distress, it can begin to organize perception, relationship, and behavior. This does not mean the person is "an angry person." It means the nervous system has learned to rely on a narrow pathway under stress.

Anger is not always loud. It can be expressed through withdrawal, contempt, silence, passive resistance, moral judgment, or guilt. It can be held until the "right time," turned inward as self-attack, or discharged explosively when activation surpasses tolerance. The form differs. The function is often the same: anger becomes a way to manage vulnerability.

What Anger Protects

Anger often protects against emotions that feel more threatening than anger itself. For many people, anger is easier than sadness, fear, shame, helplessness, or longing. Anger creates movement through energy. It offers clarity. It produces a sense of power in moments when power feels uncertain.

When the underlying emotion is grief, anger may appear as irritability or contempt. When the underlying emotion is fear, anger may appear as aggression or control. When the underlying emotion is shame, anger may appear as blame. When the underlying emotion is longing, anger may appear as resentment.

In this way, anger can function like armor. It may keep the person from feeling exposed, dependent, or vulnerable. It may keep others at a distance. It may prevent the experience of needing something that might not be received.

The Nervous System and the Speed of Anger

Anger does not arise only from thought. It arises from the nervous system. When the body registers threat, it mobilizes for action. Heart rate increases. Muscles tense. Attention narrows. The mind becomes focused on perceived injustice or danger. In these moments, reflection becomes difficult.

For some individuals, anger arrives with little warning because the nervous system moves quickly from baseline to high arousal. The person may not notice early signs of activation—tightening in the chest, changes in breathing, a subtle sense of urgency—until anger is already intense. Once fully activated, the capacity to pause, interpret, and choose response is significantly reduced.

Once activation passes a certain threshold, cognitive processing narrows and behavior becomes reactive rather than reflective.

This does not mean change is impossible. It means change must occur earlier than the explosion. It also means that regulation is not simply a matter of willpower. It is a matter of awareness, practice, and the development of alternative pathways.

Why Common Advice Often Fails

Much popular advice about anger focuses on suppression ("calm down," "let it go") or discharge ("vent," "get it out"). For many, these approaches are ineffective because they address expression rather than function.

Suppression increases internal pressure. Discharge can provide brief relief but often strengthens the pathway by rehearsing it. Advice that validates anger without cultivating regulation can also be problematic. When people are encouraged to express anger freely without learning how to stay present, tolerate discomfort, and communicate effectively, anger becomes more entrenched.

If anger has become a primary regulatory tool, the goal cannot be simply to eliminate it. The goal must be to understand what it has been doing—and to develop other ways of doing that work.

How Anger Becomes Identity

When anger is repeatedly relied upon, it can begin to shape identity. People may come to see themselves as "the one who is always wronged," "the one who has to fight," "the one who has to keep score," "the one who has to hold everything together," or "the one who must stay quiet to keep the peace."

In these identities, anger serves a role. It creates coherence. It provides predictability. It offers a sense of protection—even when it damages relationships.

Because anger often feels justified, it is especially difficult to examine. People may believe that if they stop being angry, they will become vulnerable to exploitation or loss. Anger becomes associated with self-respect. Letting go becomes associated with surrender.

This is why anger patterns persist long after the conditions that shaped them have changed.

Over time, what began as adaptation becomes identity. The individual no longer experiences anger as a strategy they use, but as a reflection of who they are. The pattern becomes self-confirming.

Explosive Anger

Explosive anger is the most visible form. It erupts quickly, overwhelms both the individual and others, and often leaves confusion, remorse, or exhaustion in its wake. To observers, it may appear disproportionate or unpredictable. To the person experiencing it, it feels immediate and justified and remorseful afterward.

Explosive anger does not begin as aggression. It begins as distress that could not be regulated safely. Children who grow up in environments where mistakes are punished harshly, emotions are dismissed, or caregivers are unpredictable may learn to suppress feelings until they become intolerable. When regulation fails, intensity replaces expression.

This form of anger is dramatic, but not necessarily the most destructive. Its visibility at least invites recognition. The quieter patterns often go unchallenged for far longer.

Beneath explosive anger is often shame—the painful sense of being flawed, exposed, or inadequate. Anger provides temporary relief from that vulnerability by shifting attention outward. The explosion is not only discharge; it is defense.

These patterns are not diagnoses or fixed identities. They are adaptive strategies—ways individuals learned to manage threat, maintain connection, or preserve a sense of self. Most people rely on more than one pattern depending on context.

Understanding them provides a map. Without such a map, anger appears chaotic and unpredictable. With it, previously confusing interactions begin to make sense.

The chapters that follow examine each pattern in depth—its origins, its emotional logic, its relational impact, and the pathways through which change becomes possible.

Early Roots

The roots of anger patterns are typically found in early relational experience. Children learn not only whether anger is permitted, but how it affects connection.

In some families, anger is explosive and unpredictable. In others, it is ignored or punished. In still others, it is expressed indirectly through guilt, withdrawal, or martyrdom. Each environment teaches a different lesson about what anger means and how it should be managed.

Shame As Hidden Fuel

Shame often operates as the unseen accelerant of anger. While anger focuses outward—on injustice, frustration, or threat—shame focuses inward, generating beliefs of defectiveness, inadequacy, or unworthiness.

When shame is activated, anger may emerge to counteract the intolerable sense of exposure or vulnerability. Alternatively, anger may be suppressed to avoid further rejection. In either case, shame intensifies the emotional landscape, making reactions feel urgent and disproportionate.

Because shame is difficult to acknowledge directly, it frequently remains hidden beneath more visible emotions. Understanding its role helps explain why anger sometimes appears disconnected from the immediate situation.

Children adapt accordingly. They develop strategies that maximize safety and belonging within their particular situation. These strategies become embodied—not merely ideas, but patterns of perception, emotion, and behavior.

Over time, what began as adaptation becomes identity.

The Build-Up No One Sees—Kay

Anger rarely begins as rage.

It begins as small signals.

A tightening in the chest. A flash of irritation. A brief sense of unfairness. These signals often appear quietly and disappear quickly, especially when maintaining harmony feels more important than acknowledging discomfort.

Most people override these signals without noticing. They reassure themselves that the moment is not important, that someone else did not mean what it seemed they meant, that reacting would only make things worse.

Each time this happens the signal fades, but the underlying tension remains.

Over time these moments accumulate. What appears later as sudden anger is often the result of many small experiences that were dismissed or ignored. The final reaction may seem disproportionate to the immediate situation because the situation is not the real source of the feeling.

By the time anger becomes visible, the build-up has already occurred.

Kay, for instance, did not see herself as an angry person. She described herself as "high-strung" and easily frustrated. Her family, however, described something different.

A minor disagreement about dinner plans could escalate rapidly. A misplaced bill, a forgotten errand, a slow computer—each could ignite an outburst that left everyone in the household tense and silent. Afterward, Kay would often apologize, sometimes tearfully, insisting she had been under too much stress.

What Kay did not recognize was the accumulation beneath the surface. She had grown up in a home where mistakes were harshly criticized and emotional expression was unsafe. She learned to monitor herself constantly. When that control slipped—even briefly—the release was intense.

Her anger was not random. It was organized around shame and fear of inadequacy.

Guilt-Based Anger

While explosive anger is visible and outwardly disruptive, other forms of anger operate through connection rather than rupture. Instead of pushing others away, they draw others in—often through responsibility or emotional pressure.

This is the domain of guilt-based anger.

Guilt-based anger is less obvious but often more enduring. It organizes relationships around responsibility rather than reciprocity. While explosive anger pushes others away, guilt-based anger pulls others close—but through obligation rather than mutual choice.

This form of anger operates through guilt rather than confrontation. Here anger is expressed by inducing responsibility in others or by absorbing blame oneself. The individual may appear fragile, self-sacrificing, or excessively conscientious.

Because guilt maintains connection without overt conflict, this pattern can persist for decades before its underlying anger is recognized.

Guilt Inducer / Guilt Absorber

Unlike explosive anger, which seeks release, guilt-based anger organizes around connection. Two complementary roles frequently emerge.

The guilt inducer expresses disappointment, hurt, or moral authority in ways that create pressure for others to respond.

The guilt absorber experiences intense discomfort when others are upset and moves quickly to repair, appease, or take responsibility.

These roles frequently emerge together within families and relationships, reinforcing one another over time until the pattern feels normal, even inevitable.

How the Pairing Forms

Anger patterns rarely exist in isolation. They interact with complementary patterns in others, forming relational pairings that feel strangely familiar and difficult to change.

One partner may escalate while the other withdraws. One may induce guilt while the other absorbs it. One may retaliate while the other seeks appeasement. Each behavior reinforces the other, creating a self-sustaining system.

These pairings are not random. They reflect compatible strategies learned earlier in life. The relationship feels compelling because it recreates familiar emotional terrain, even when it is painful.

Guilt-based anger often develops in environments where love feels conditional and emotional security depends on maintaining harmony.

Children may learn that expressing needs creates distress for caregivers, while attending to others 'needs preserves connection. Some adopt the role of emotional caretaker; others learn to influence through disappointment or sacrifice.

These roles stabilize the family system but constrain individual development. Meet Marsha.

Marsha

Marsha prided herself on being devoted to her family. She managed the household meticulously, anticipated everyone's needs, and rarely asked for anything directly.

When family members failed to meet her expectations, she did not erupt. Instead, she became subdued and withdrawn. Her silence communicated injury more powerfully than words.

Her sadness functioned as accusation. Her suffering demanded response. Obligation replaced choice.

Her anger was expressed through disappointment rather than confrontation. Meet her partner, Carol.

Carol

Carol occupied the complementary role. She felt acutely uncomfortable when someone close to her was upset. Even mild disapproval triggered anxiety.

To restore harmony, she worked harder, gave more, and suppressed her own needs. Over time, she lost clarity about her own preferences. Maintaining peace became her organizing principle.

Why the Dynamic Persists

Over time, guilt-based interactions become self-reinforcing. The inducer experiences validation when others respond with concern or accommodation. The absorber experiences relief when tension decreases.

Relationships organized around guilt may appear close yet lack true mutuality.

Once established, anger pairings are remarkably stable. Attempts to change often provoke anxiety, because the pattern—however problematic—has provided predictability.

If one partner alters their behavior, the other may escalate efforts to restore the familiar equilibrium. Without awareness, both individuals may conclude that change is impossible or that the problem lies solely within one person.

Understanding the system rather than assigning blame opens the possibility of movement.

Attachment Patterns That Give Rise to Guilt-Based Anger

Attachment theory provides a framework for understanding these dynamics. Early experiences with caregivers shape expectations about availability, responsiveness, and safety. These expectations become internal working models that guide adult relationships.

Individuals who learned that closeness was unreliable may remain vigilant for signs of rejection. Those who learned that autonomy was discouraged may fear separation. Anger often emerges at moments when these attachment concerns are activated.

Guilt-based anger develops within relationships where emotional boundaries are unclear and responsibility is unevenly distributed.

Children who assume emotional responsibility for caregivers may become adults who experience others 'distress as intolerable. Conversely, those whose needs were met primarily through sacrifice may learn to influence through self-denial or disappointment.

A Common Relational Scenario—Ellen & David

Consider a situation in which one partner feels neglected and expresses frustration. The other experiences this as criticism and withdraws. The withdrawal intensifies the first partner's anxiety, leading to stronger protest. The cycle escalates, with each person reacting to the other's response rather than the original issue.

Neither intends harm. Both are attempting to restore security using familiar strategies. Without awareness, the pattern repeats across topics and over time.

Ellen expressed disappointment when David prioritized work or personal interests. David responded by apologizing and adjusting, often abandoning his own preferences.

Resentment accumulated quietly on both sides. Neither recognized the pattern as anger. It appeared instead as love, responsibility, and duty.

Passive Anger

Not all anger seeks confrontation. Some seeks invisibility.

Passive anger operates through avoidance, delay, inefficiency, or withdrawal. It allows resistance without overt conflict.

Passive anger is among the least recognized forms of anger because it rarely looks like anger at all. It is expressed indirectly, through delay, withdrawal, forgetfulness, inefficiency, compliance followed by resentment, or physical distress. The individual often experiences themselves not as angry, but as overwhelmed, misunderstood, or unfairly burdened.

In passive anger, direct expression feels unsafe. Open conflict threatens connection, approval, or stability. As a result, anger goes underground, emerging sideways rather than head-on. Commitments are missed; energy falters, enthusiasm fades, and others are left confused about what went wrong.

Because the anger is not acknowledged, both parties experience frustration without clarity. The passive individual feels imposed upon and unappreciated; others experience them as unreliable or disengaged. Neither sees the full picture.

This pattern often develops in environments where anger was discouraged or punished, and where compliance was rewarded. The child learned that maintaining harmony required suppressing dissatisfaction. Over time, suppression gave way to indirect expression.

Passive anger preserves connection in the short term but erodes trust in the long term. Needs remain unspoken, resentment accumulates, and relationships become organized around disappointment rather than collaboration. Below is an illustration of these themes.

Marge

Marge sat in my office with the posture of someone who had endured too much. She was in her late forties, neatly dressed, her hands folded carefully in her lap. Her voice was calm, but the tension in her jaw suggested that calm was a practiced state rather than a natural one.

"I'm not an angry person," she began. "I'm just tired of being treated like I don't matter."

Marge described a marriage in which she felt dismissed and taken for granted. Her husband, she said, was not cruel. He simply moved through life as if her needs were optional. When she asked for help, he "forgot." When she expressed disappointment, he minimized it. Over time, Marge stopped asking.

She did not yell. She did not confront. Instead, she withdrew emotionally, becoming polite and distant. She stopped initiating affection. She stopped sharing her inner life. She began to "forget" his preferences, ignore his requests, and respond with a flat neutrality that made him increasingly anxious.

"I don't know why he's so upset," she said with a faint smile. "I'm fine."

It became clear that Marge's anger had not disappeared. It had been redirected—expressed through disengagement rather than confrontation. Her withdrawal protected her from disappointment, but it also became a form of punishment. The relationship was no longer a shared space. It had become a battleground of distance.

Marge did not experience her behavior as hostile. She experienced it as survival. Similarly, meet Tim.

Tim

Tim appeared agreeable and cooperative, yet projects involving him frequently stalled. Deadlines were missed, details overlooked, commitments forgotten.

Raised in an environment where open disagreement led to escalation, he learned compliance on the surface and resistance underneath.

His anger was expressed through inaction rather than opposition.

Retaliatory Anger

Retaliatory anger organizes around fairness and restoration of balance. Injuries are remembered rather than discharged.

Retaliatory anger differs sharply from both explosive and passive forms. It is not immediate and not hidden—it is stored. Grievances are remembered, cataloged, and revisited. Injury is not discharged; it is held in reserve.

Individuals organized around retaliatory anger often experience the world through the lens of fairness and justice. Slights are magnified, motives scrutinized, and balance carefully monitored. Forgiveness feels risky, as though it invites further harm.

Expression is delayed but precise. Confrontations may occur long after the triggering event, delivered with detailed recollection and moral certainty. Others experience these moments as disproportionate or unexpected; the individual experiences them as measured and justified.

This pattern frequently develops in environments where harm went unacknowledged or accountability was inconsistent. Children learned that direct appeal was ineffective and that protection depended on vigilance and memory.

Over time, the ability to remember injury becomes equated with safety. Letting go may feel not like forgiveness but like surrendering protection.

Retaliatory anger restores a sense of power but constrains intimacy. Relationships become conditional, shaped by tests of loyalty and fairness. Repair is difficult once judgment has been rendered. Stephanie embodies these concepts.

Stephanie

Stephanie described keeping careful mental records of slights. She rarely confronted others immediately but waited until she felt certain of her position.

"I don't forget," she said evenly. "I just wait."

Retaliation restored a sense of justice, even if it prolonged conflict. Relationships became guarded. Others sensed her vigilance but could not always name it.

She experienced herself as principled, not hostile.

How Anger Becomes a Worldview

When anger patterns are reinforced repeatedly, they can extend beyond relationships into a broader interpretation of reality.

The world begins to appear hostile, unfair, unpredictable, or dismissive, depending on the individual's history.

Information that confirms this worldview is noticed and remembered. Contradictory experiences may be discounted. Over time, the worldview feels self-evident.

When anger persists over time, it shapes expectations about relationships. Anger is no longer episodic; it becomes part of how the world is interpreted.

Life-Stance Anger

For some individuals, anger becomes a lens through which the world is viewed. Disappointment is expected. Trust is guarded. Vigilance becomes identity.

Life-stance anger is not limited to specific episodes or relationships. It becomes a worldview—a generalized orientation toward life itself. The individual may not appear overtly angry, yet experiences the world as frustrating, disappointing, or fundamentally unjust.

This pattern develops gradually, often through repeated experiences of helplessness, loss, or chronic stress. Rather than responding to discrete events, anger becomes the background tone of existence. Irritability, cynicism, and chronic dissatisfaction replace acute outbursts.

Because it is diffuse, life-stance anger is difficult to confront directly. There is no single incident to resolve, no clear antagonist.

The individual may attribute their mood to circumstances, personality, or the state of the world, rarely recognizing the underlying emotional continuity.

Relationships with those organized around life-stance anger can feel draining or hopeless. Efforts to improve conditions are dismissed as temporary or inadequate. Positivity may be interpreted as naïve; concern as intrusive.

At its core, this pattern reflects adaptation to prolonged disempowerment. Anger becomes less a response than a posture—a way of bracing against further disappointment. This was Charles ' way.

Charles—The Quiet Costs

Charles seated himself opposite me in the office, ready to begin his first session. He didn't wait for any ice breakers. "OK, Doc, let's get one thing straight. I sure as hell don't belong here, cause I'm not crazy, so don't try to give me a lot of psycho-babble crap." A small powerfully built man, Charles had given a clue to his hostility by shaking hands as if trying to crush my hand in a vise. His walk was a kind of swagger, and his whole manner was that of a man with a gigantic chip on his shoulder. It was evident that Charles was ready to do battle with a hostile world. Expecting the worst, his history indicated that he usually got it.

His confrontational stance had resulted in the loss of many jobs and a catastrophic personal life. He described himself as realistic. He trusted few people and expected incompetence or betrayal.

His stance protected him from vulnerability, but it also limited intimacy and joy.

"Me against them," was Charles 'motto.

Isolation became the price of safety.

The stance that once protected him from humiliation had gradually become the structure of his life.

Attachment & The Internal Working Model

Repeated relational experiences form internal working models—expectations about self, others, and the world.

If early relationships were unpredictable, critical, or emotionally demanding, anger may become an organizing tool for managing uncertainty.

Understanding one's internal working model allows previously puzzling reactions to become coherent.

Why Anger Makes Sense

Perhaps the most important principle of this book is that anger always makes sense in context. Even when behavior is destructive or confusing, it reflects an attempt to solve a problem or protect something of value.

Understanding the purpose of anger does not excuse harmful actions, but it allows compassion and responsibility to coexist.

Anger rarely appears without purpose. It protects against vulnerability, signals injustice, mobilizes action, or preserves identity.

Understanding anger as adaptation does not excuse harm. It clarifies it.

When individuals recognize how their anger developed and what it has been trying to accomplish, they gain the freedom to choose new responses. When anger is understood, it becomes possible to choose differently.

The goal is not to eliminate anger, but to integrate it—transforming it from a rigid reflex into a flexible signal.

A Framework for Change

Change begins with curiosity rather than condemnation. The question is not "How do I stop being angry?" The question is "What is my anger doing for me, and what does it cost?"

Once the function is understood, the work becomes expanding options. This includes:

- *learning to notice early activation cues*
- *building tolerance for uncomfortable emotions that anger often covers*
- *developing language for boundaries, needs, disappointment, and fear*
- *practicing interruption before escalation becomes inevitable*
- *replacing old strategies with new forms of regulation and repair*

Repair within relationships often becomes the testing ground where new responses replace familiar anger patterns.

Anger is not the enemy. It is information—and often a form of protection. When its purpose is understood, it no longer has to dictate behavior.

Because anger patterns are structural, meaningful change requires more than behavioral control. It involves developing new ways of regulating distress, interpreting experience, and relating to others.

Meaningful change does not occur through willpower alone. Because anger patterns are embedded in perception, emotion, and physiology, intervention must address the underlying structure— increasing awareness, tolerance of discomfort, and flexibility in response.

Small shifts can alter entire relational systems when sustained over time.

Change is possible, but it occurs gradually as new experiences challenge old expectations.

Closing Reflection

Anger is easy to misinterpret, both in ourselves and in others. We often see only the expression and miss the function. We judge the volume and miss the fear beneath it. We condemn the behavior and miss the history that shaped it.

This book is not an argument for suppressing anger. It is an invitation to understand it—how it formed, what it protects, and how it can be integrated rather than acted out.

When anger becomes one of many available responses rather than the only response, the nervous system regains flexibility. Relationships regain possibility. And the self is no longer organized around defense.

Anger is not the enemy. It is a messenger shaped by history and experience.

When individuals begin to understand the architecture of their anger—how it formed, what it protects, and why it persists—the emotion itself becomes less frightening and more informative. The goal is not to eliminate anger, but to free it from patterns that no longer serve.

The chapters that follow examine specific anger patterns in depth, exploring how each develops, how it operates, and how change becomes possible.

Understanding precedes transformation.

CHAPTER TWO

DISILLUSIONMENT & RECALIBRATION

Anger often persists not because people want to be angry, but because the strategies they have been given to manage it do not work. Many individuals arrive at this stage after years of effort—reading, attending workshops, trying techniques, and attempting to follow well-intentioned advice. When relief fails to materialize, frustration deepens into discouragement. What begins as a search for control becomes a recognition that something more fundamental is missing.

Many people arrive at this moment quietly.

There is rarely a dramatic realization that something is wrong. Instead, there is a gradual accumulation of frustration. Techniques that once seemed promising begin to feel mechanical. Advice that once sounded wise begins to feel strangely hollow.

Individuals may notice themselves repeating the same internal questions:

Why does this keep happening?

Why do I understand what I'm supposed to do but still react the same way?

Why does anger feel so immediate even when I know it causes damage?

These questions do not signal failure. They signal readiness.

Disillusionment marks the point at which a person stops trying to control anger solely through effort or willpower and begins to examine the deeper system that generates it.

That shift—from management to understanding—is the beginning of recalibration.

When familiar solutions stop working, attention shifts from managing surface behavior to understanding underlying patterns. The goal is no longer simply to reduce anger, but to understand what anger has been doing—what needs it has served, what vulnerabilities it has protected, and why it continues to arise even when it causes harm.

Jerry

Jerry did not describe himself as an angry man. In fact, he insisted that anger was not really the problem. What troubled him, he said, was that nothing seemed to work anymore. Techniques he had been taught to "manage anger" left him feeling either artificially restrained or explosively out of control.

He had attended workshops, read self-help books, and tried various methods of releasing tension. For a time, some of these strategies seemed helpful. But the relief never lasted. Each episode left him feeling more discouraged, as though the real issue remained untouched.

Jerry did not suffer from anger as a singular emotion. Rather, anger had become his primary way of organizing distress—a familiar pathway activated whenever he felt overwhelmed, threatened, or powerless.

The turning point came when he began to suspect that the problem was not simply "too much anger," but a reliance on anger as his only reliable regulatory tool. If anger was the only language available, then removing it without replacing it would leave him effectively voiceless.

This realization marked the beginning of disillusionment—not with himself, but with approaches that addressed behavior without addressing the underlying system.

What Jerry began to recognize is something many people eventually discover: anger is not simply an emotion that appears at random.

For some individuals it functions as a regulatory shortcut.

When distress rises—fear, humiliation, disappointment, helplessness—anger organizes the experience quickly. It converts diffuse emotional discomfort into a focused state of activation. The body mobilizes. Attention sharpens. The mind begins searching for cause and responsibility.

In that moment anger can feel stabilizing.

But when anger becomes the primary way of regulating distress, other emotional capacities begin to narrow. Vulnerability becomes harder to tolerate. Reflection slows. Relationships become arenas of defense rather than connection.

What looks like "too much anger" is often something more specific: too few alternative ways of managing emotional pain.

Why Common Advice About Anger Fails—and What Actually Helps

Much of the advice given about anger assumes that the goal is either suppression ("calm down," "let it go") or discharge ("get it out," "vent your feelings"). For individuals whose anger operates as a deeply ingrained pattern, both approaches can be ineffective or even counterproductive.

Suppression increases internal pressure, making later explosions more likely. Unstructured discharge may provide momentary relief but often rehearses the neural and behavioral pathways that sustain the pattern.

Approaches that provide validation without containment are particularly problematic. When individuals are encouraged to express anger freely without developing regulation skills or reflective capacity, anger can become more entrenched rather than less.

To expand beyond reliance on anger, it is necessary to understand what anger has been doing—what functions it has served—and to develop alternative ways of meeting those needs.

Alice & Anthony

Alice and Anthony sought counseling because their arguments had become relentless. Each session seemed to devolve into the same pattern: escalating accusations, defensive counterattacks, and emotional exhaustion.

Alice described Anthony as domineering and intimidating. Anthony described Alice as hypersensitive and impossible to satisfy. Both felt misunderstood; both felt victimized.

In prior counseling, they had been encouraged to "express their feelings openly." What followed was not resolution but intensification. Each learned to articulate grievances more forcefully, but neither developed the capacity to listen or regulate.

Their conflicts were not about a single issue. They reflected incompatible strategies for managing distress. Anthony escalated to assert control; Alice escalated to secure reassurance. The louder the exchange, the less either felt heard.

The difficulty with advice to "communicate more" becomes apparent when one or both partners are organized around winning rather than understanding. Without a framework for regulation and mutual recognition, communication itself can become another arena for conflict.

Couples often assume that conflict arises because partners disagree about specific issues—money, time, responsibilities, parenting.

Yet in many relationships the disagreement itself is not the central problem.

The difficulty lies in how each partner manages emotional activation once conflict begins.

Some individuals escalate in order to gain control or force recognition. Others withdraw in order to reduce overwhelm. Still others attempt to soothe or placate to restore stability.

When these strategies collide, each partner inadvertently intensifies the other's anxiety.

One becomes louder.

The other becomes quieter.

One pursues harder.

The other retreats further.

Both feel increasingly alone inside the same conversation.

Effective couples work therefore focuses less on solving the surface problem and more on helping partners remain emotionally present while the problem is discussed.

What Effective Couples Work Does Differently

Effective couples work does not simply encourage expression; it cultivates the capacity to remain present in the face of strong emotion. Partners learn to recognize physiological arousal, pause before reacting, and shift from accusation to description.

Listening becomes an active skill rather than a passive stance. Individuals practice tracking both their own internal states and their partner's experience, even when those experiences diverge sharply.

This process is difficult. It is not a matter of flipping a switch but of adjusting a rheostat—gradually increasing tolerance for vulnerability and ambiguity. Progress often occurs unevenly, with setbacks that can feel discouraging. Yet over time, the relational climate can shift from adversarial to collaborative.

Repair of attachment injuries—the underlying fears of abandonment, rejection, or domination—becomes possible only when both partners experience sufficient safety to lower defensive intensity.

Jayne

Jayne sought help after a series of ruptured relationships left her feeling bewildered and alone. She described herself as someone who "gave everything" yet repeatedly ended up in volatile partnerships.

During conflicts, Jayne reported feeling flooded with emotion—a mixture of anger, fear, and desperation. Her responses alternated between intense pursuit and abrupt withdrawal. Afterward, she often felt ashamed and uncertain how the situation had escalated so quickly.

Jayne had previously been advised to "release her anger" rather than hold it in. She tried this approach, expressing grievances forcefully in the hope that honesty would lead to clarity. Instead, her partners experienced her intensity as attack, prompting defensive reactions that confirmed her fears of abandonment.

What Jayne needed was not greater expression but greater regulation—the ability to remain connected to herself while communicating distress. Without that capacity, attempts at openness simply amplified the cycle.

Why Venting Fails

While expression can be healthy when guided by awareness and containment, unstructured venting often has the opposite effect.

Anger mobilizes the body for action. Repeatedly activating this state without resolution strengthens the neural pathways associated with hostility and arousal. Individuals may experience temporary relief after an outburst, but the underlying system remains primed for future activation.

For some, venting becomes a ritual that reinforces identity as an aggrieved or embattled person. Rather than dissipating anger, it rehearses it.

One reason venting can become so reinforcing is that anger often sits on top of other emotional states.

Beneath anger there may be grief about a disappointment that cannot be undone.

There may be fear about losing influence or belonging.

There may be shame about feeling inadequate or exposed.

Beliefs emerge that prompt a reactions, such as:

Someone is wrong.

Something is unfair.

Action is required.

This clarity can feel powerful, but it also prevents deeper emotional processing. When anger dominates the system, quieter emotions struggle to find expression.

Learning to pause inside anger long enough to identify what lies beneath it is one of the most important steps in expanding emotional flexibility.

To move beyond reliance on anger, individuals must develop skills that reduce baseline activation and increase tolerance for uncomfortable feelings such as sadness, fear, or disappointment—emotions that anger often masks.

Children, Anger & Power

Patterns of anger are frequently rooted in early experiences with power and vulnerability. Children who feel chronically powerless may discover that anger produces results—attention, compliance, distance, or relief from overwhelming demands.

Conversely, children exposed to unpredictable or threatening environments may learn that anger is necessary for self-protection. Over time, these strategies become automatic, persisting long after the original circumstances have changed. In some families, anger is the only emotion that produces movement. Sadness is ignored. Fear is dismissed. Requests are postponed. But anger – loud and persistent – cannot be overlooked.

The Child learns that anger works. In other families, anger is forbidden. Children are expected to be compliant and emotionally controlled. In these homes anger goes underground, emerging indirectly through sarcasm, withdrawal, guilt or self-blame. In both cases, anger becomes functional long before it becomes problematic. It regulates distress and organizes relationships.

What is rarely taught is how to experience anger without being driven by it. Without opportunities to learn alternative forms of regulation, the individual's repertoire remains narrow. Anger becomes the most accessible response, even when it undermines long-term goals.

Change, Attachment Repair, and the Reality of the Work

Therapeutic work is rarely dramatic and rarely quick. Change occurs gradually through repeated moments of awareness, interruption, and choice.

For individuals whose nervous systems learned early that intensity was necessary for survival, quiet can feel unfamiliar – even threatening. Slowing down may initially increase anxiety rather than relieve it. From an attachment perspective, this work is reparative precisely because it unfolds within relationship. Each time a partner remains present rather than attacking or withdrawing, a new expectation forms. Each time distress is met with responsiveness rather than escalation, the body learns that connection can be sustained without force.

These moments accumulate. Slowly, the internal working model begins to shift.

Transition to Self-Reflection

Understanding the origins and functions of anger can be illuminating, but insight alone does not change patterns. Individuals often benefit from concrete ways to assess how strongly anger operates in their own lives.

Patterns of anger are often invisible to the person experiencing them.

Because anger can feel justified in the moment, it rarely appears to the individual as a pattern. Each episode seems tied to a specific circumstance—an unfair comment, a frustrating delay, a perceived insult.

Over time, however, certain tendencies begin to repeat.

The following checklist invites you to look for patterns that may otherwise remain hidden in everyday life.

It is not a diagnostic tool. It is an invitation to curiosity—a means of recognizing tendencies that may otherwise feel invisible or "just the way things are."

Anger Checklist: Reliance on Anger

Consider whether you frequently:

- Feel a surge of energy or clarity when angry
- Experience difficulty calming down once activated
- Replay conflicts repeatedly in your mind
- Interpret ambiguous situations as hostile or unfair
- Feel justified in responses that later cause regret

- Use anger to avoid feeling vulnerable or helpless
- Experience physical tension, headaches, or fatigue after conflicts
- Notice that relationships become strained during periods of stress
- Feel that others do not take you seriously unless you are forceful
- Alternate between suppression and explosive expression
- Feel ashamed or depleted after episodes of anger
- Struggle to express needs without irritation
- Become impatient with perceived incompetence or inefficiency
- Feel driven to "win" arguments
- Withdraw abruptly after conflicts
- Experience difficulty trusting others 'intentions
- Feel misunderstood even when you have explained yourself
- Sense that anger is both familiar and exhausting

Answering "yes" to several items does not define you. It suggests that anger may have become a familiar way of managing distress—a pattern worth understanding more fully.

How to Understand Your Responses

Patterns matter more than totals. Occasional anger is normal; persistent reliance on anger as the primary coping mechanism can narrow emotional flexibility and relational options.

Recognizing this reliance is not a cause for self-criticism. It is an opportunity to expand the range of responses available when distress arises.

Toward Change

Real change in patterns of anger rarely begins with control.

Many people arrive at this point after years of trying to suppress, manage, or eliminate their reactions. When those efforts fail, the experience can feel discouraging. Yet this moment of frustration often signals the beginning of a different kind of work.

Instead of asking how to stop anger, the question shifts toward understanding what anger has been doing.

Anger often develops as a solution to a problem that once felt overwhelming. It may have protected against humiliation, defended against vulnerability, or created a sense of control in situations that felt chaotic or threatening. What once served a purpose can gradually become automatic, appearing even when the original conditions have long since changed.

Recognizing this does not excuse harmful behavior. But it does restore clarity. Anger begins to appear less as a defect to eliminate and more as a signal pointing toward something unfinished.

This shift requires patience.

Patterns that develop over many years rarely dissolve quickly. Individuals often notice that awareness grows faster than change.

They may begin to recognize familiar reactions even as they continue to experience them. This stage can feel uncomfortable, yet it represents an important transition.

Observation gradually interrupts automaticity.

Moments that once passed unnoticed begin to stand out. The surge of energy before an argument. The tightening in the body that signals rising frustration. The familiar internal narrative that frames situations as unfair or threatening.

These small recognitions create space.

In that space, anger can begin to serve a different function. Instead of directing behavior immediately, it becomes information—an indication that something meaningful is occurring inside the person or within the relationship.

Understanding does not eliminate anger. But it changes the relationship to it.

And from that shift, new possibilities begin to emerge.

Closing Reflection

Disillusionment with ineffective strategies can feel discouraging, yet it also creates space for recalibration. When individuals stop trying to eliminate anger and begin trying to understand it, new possibilities emerge.

Anger is not the enemy. It is a signal—one that points toward unmet needs, perceived threats, or unresolved pain. Learning to interpret that signal rather than react automatically to it is the beginning of change, but anger does not speak in only one voice.

It appears in different forms, shaped by the ways individuals have learned to protect themselves, assert power, or preserve connection. Understanding these patterns—the languages anger uses to communicate—reveals why certain reactions repeat and why others remain difficult to express.

The chapters that follow explore these anger languages more closely, showing how each one develops, how it operates within relationships, and how learning to recognize them opens the door to different choices.

CHAPTER THREE

PASSIVE ANGER

When Anger Goes Underground

Not all anger announces itself. Some of the most enduring and costly forms of anger are the ones that remain hidden—contained beneath politeness, humor, or apparent compliance. These quieter expressions of anger often go unnoticed for years, even by those who carry them.

Unlike explosive anger, which disrupts relationships visibly, passive anger operates through subtle patterns that preserve connection on the surface while expressing resistance underneath. The result is a style of coping that can appear cooperative, reasonable, or even self-sacrificing, yet leaves both the individual and others confused about what is actually happening.

Passive anger represents one of the most common anger languages. Instead of speaking anger openly, the individual communicates through delay, forgetfulness, withdrawal, illness, or helplessness. The message is still there—but it is encoded in behavior rather than words.

Nancy & Jeff

Nancy rarely thought of herself as angry. She was reliable, accommodating, and often the one others turned to when something needed to get done. When Jeff asked if she could take care of a few things he hadn't had time for, she agreed before she fully registered the request. She smiled as she said yes, adding, "It's fine," even as something tightened briefly in her chest.

Jeff noticed her compliance but not the effort it required. From his perspective, things worked smoothly between them. Nancy rarely complained, and when she did, it was often softened with humor or followed by reassurance that it wasn't a big deal.

Later that evening, Nancy felt restless and irritable, though nothing obvious had gone wrong. She told herself she was being unreasonable. After all, she hadn't been forced. She had chosen to help. Still, a quiet resentment lingered, accompanied by fatigue she couldn't quite explain.

When Jeff asked what was wrong, Nancy hesitated, then shook her head. "Nothing," she said. The word felt familiar. So did the knot in her stomach.

It was only much later—long after similar moments had accumulated—that Nancy began to recognize what she had missed in those early exchanges: the fleeting signals her body offered before she agreed, the wishes she dismissed before they reached language. The anger was never loud enough to be recognized, but it had been there all along.

Over time, these quiet concessions accumulate. What begins as momentary self-suppression can evolve into patterns of behavior that express anger indirectly—through fatigue, irritability, or resistance that neither party fully understands.

Passive Anger in Action

Emily burst through my office door, threw herself breathlessly onto the couch, bounced back up to hand me a crumpled envelope, then settled more slowly into her seat. She glanced at a colorful watch that went with her navy Lululemon athletic set and Hoka running shoes.

"Wouldn't you know it, I stop to put on my walking shoes and now I'm twenty minutes late. If you'll just open that envelope, it'll save me a lot of time telling you why I'm here. That's what you want to know, right?"

The envelope contained a counseling referral from Emily's supervisor. According to him, Emily was on probation for chronic lateness, missed meetings and appointments, lack of follow-through on projects, and a generally blasé attitude toward her work.

I watched her out of the corner of my eye as I read the report aloud. At first she seemed surprised. Then, slowly, her demeanor shifted. The exuberant woman who had entered my office became quiet and brittle, like a child bracing for disappointment.

When she spoke, it was with a high, light tone and an awkward smile.

"I can't believe Jerry could say those things—that I could lose my job over such trivia. It's not true, none of it. I'm always nice to that creep. I never let him know what I'm really thinking. Ask anyone at work. They'll all tell you I'm a good worker. Everybody likes me."

"Why do you suppose Jerry would write such things, then?" I asked.

"Oh, that's just him. He's so demanding. And worse than that, he's a perfectionist. I'll never be able to please him. I'm not perfect, you know. Oh, why does this always happen to me?"

As Emily talked, it became increasingly clear that she was furious—but not in a way she could acknowledge or express directly. Her anger showed itself instead through chronic lateness, missed commitments, and a pattern of passive resistance that had now placed her job in jeopardy.

Emily did not experience herself as angry. She prided herself on being pleasant, agreeable, and easy to get along with. She smiled often, laughed readily, and avoided open conflict whenever possible. Yet beneath that smile was a reservoir of resentment that leaked out sideways.

Her supervisor experienced her behavior as irresponsible and disrespectful. Emily experienced her supervisor as demanding and impossible to please. Neither view was entirely wrong. But the absence of direct communication ensured the conflict would continue unresolved.

Passive anger often carries the experience of being a victim of unreasonable demands, where resentment accumulates quietly rather than being expressed directly.

Meet Meredith

She agreed before she realized she had.

It was a small request—covering a shift, staying late, taking on one more task. She smiled as she said yes, even heard herself sound reassuring. "No problem," she added, automatically.

Later that evening, she felt irritable and tired, though nothing in particular had gone wrong. She replayed the conversation, telling herself she shouldn't be upset—it wasn't a big deal. Others had it harder. She had chosen this.

By the end of the week, she felt resentful but couldn't quite say why. When asked what was wrong, she shrugged. "I'm fine." The words were familiar. So was the knot in her stomach.

It wasn't until much later that she recognized what she had missed in the moment she agreed: a brief tightening in her chest, a fleeting wish to say no. The anger wasn't loud enough to be recognized, but it had been there.

Moments like these rarely occur in isolation. When anger goes underground, it often becomes woven into everyday interactions, shaping relationships in ways that are easy to overlook and difficult to name.

The Smile as Armor

For many individuals who rely on passive anger, smiling preserves connection while deflecting confrontation. It reassures others that everything is fine, even when it is not.

This pattern often develops early in life. Children who learn that direct expressions of anger are met with disapproval, withdrawal, or punishment discover safer ways to cope. They become compliant, pleasant, and helpful—at least on the surface.

Anger does not disappear. It goes underground.

For many individuals organized around passive anger, the problem is not the absence of anger but the fear of what anger might do to relationships. The cost of direct expression feels too high. Compliance becomes the safer strategy.

In adulthood, this underground anger may surface through physical symptoms, chronic fatigue, depression, or vague complaints. It may also appear in relationships as missed appointments, forgotten promises, or a persistent sense that life is unfair.

Carrying the load of passive anger feels exhausting. Over time, the effort required to maintain this appearance of cooperation can exceed a person's emotional resources, leading to cycles of overcommitment followed by withdrawal, illness, or quiet collapse.

Harry: The Man Who Couldn't Say No

Harry was a quiet man in his late forties who came to therapy complaining of exhaustion. He worked long hours, volunteered for extra assignments, and was always available to help others. Friends described him as reliable and generous. His employers considered him indispensable.

Harry described his life as "overwhelming," yet he could not identify a single place where he might reduce his commitments.

"I don't mind helping out," he said quickly. "People need me. I'd feel guilty saying no."

When I asked him how he felt toward the people who made constant demands on his time, he looked genuinely puzzled.

"I don't feel anything toward them," he replied. "They're just doing what they do."

Over time, however, it became clear that Harry resented nearly everyone in his life. He arrived late to sessions, forgot appointments, and frequently complained of headaches and stomach problems. He spoke about his obligations with a weary bitterness that contrasted sharply with his cooperative demeanor.

His anger was expressed through collapse rather than confrontation. By agreeing to everything, he created conditions he could not sustain. His body eventually expressed what his words would not.

Illness as Expression

Passive anger patterns are often associated with physical symptoms, which can become the primary outlet for unexpressed rage.

Headaches, back pain, gastrointestinal problems, and chronic fatigue may appear without clear medical cause or persist beyond what would normally be expected. These symptoms are not imagined. They are real bodily experiences that often intensify during periods of interpersonal stress.

When anger cannot be acknowledged or expressed directly, the body often becomes its messenger.

These symptoms frequently serve the same regulatory function as anger itself: creating distance, interrupting demands, and protecting against further depletion.

From a developmental perspective, these patterns are not accidental. Some individuals learned early that maintaining connection required staying agreeable, minimizing distress, and avoiding expressions of anger that might disrupt fragile relationships. When caregivers were uncomfortable with anger, inconsistently responsive, or overwhelmed themselves, the child adapted by keeping emotional intensity low and needs muted.

Over time, this way of relating became embodied. Feelings that could not be acknowledged or expressed consciously did not disappear; they were carried in posture, fatigue, physical symptoms, and patterns of collapse or compliance. In such cases, the body becomes the primary messenger of psychological discomfort, expressing what words once could not.

JoAnn: Helplessness as Control

JoAnn came to therapy because her family complained she was "impossible to help." She described herself as overwhelmed and incapable of managing even simple tasks. Decisions felt paralyzing. Problems multiplied.

Yet in certain situations—especially when outcomes mattered deeply to her—JoAnn was remarkably capable.

When asked about anger, JoAnn smiled faintly.

"I don't get angry," she said softly. "I just can't cope.

Her helplessness functioned as a powerful form of control. Others stepped in, made decisions, and took responsibility for her life. Resentment simmered beneath the surface—both hers and theirs.

JoAnn's anger was not absent. It was embedded in her incapacity.

She described feeling chronically overwhelmed, yet she resisted attempts by others to encourage independence. Help was both sought and resented. Advice was dismissed as unrealistic or insensitive. Efforts to set expectations often led to further withdrawal or collapse.

In this way, JoAnn remained at the center of attention while avoiding direct confrontation. Her distress compelled others to respond, but her passivity prevented resolution.

Her behavior communicated needs she could not state directly. Anger took the form of incapacity rather than protest.

Humor as a Shield

Some individuals rely on humor to express hostility while maintaining plausible deniability. Sarcasm, teasing, and jokes allow anger to surface without being named.

"I'm just kidding," becomes a familiar refrain.

Humor can be socially acceptable and disarming, but it also creates distance. When challenged, the speaker can retreat behind the joke, leaving others uncertain whether harm was intended or imagined.

Humor becomes another dialect of anger—just disguised as playfulness.

Over time, relationships erode under the weight of these small, unacknowledged injuries. Trust weakens. Intimacy becomes difficult.

Where Passive Anger Begins

Passive anger often develops in childhood environments where direct expressions of anger were discouraged or punished. Children learned early that being agreeable and cooperative earned approval, while anger risked withdrawal or loss of affection.

In such families, anger was not resolved—it was silenced.

Children adapted by becoming compliant, helpful, or emotionally invisible. They learned to smile, to accommodate, and to take responsibility for maintaining harmony. These strategies were not pathological; they were intelligent adaptations to the emotional realities of the environment.

What was not learned was how to express anger safely and directly.

As adults, these individuals may continue to believe that anger is dangerous, even when circumstances have changed. The internal rules persist. The smile remains long after it is needed.

Why Passive Anger Is Reinforced

Passive anger is often rewarded. Others may respond with sympathy, assistance, or lowered expectations. In workplaces, these individuals may be seen as nice, easygoing, or reliable team players. In families, they may be viewed as selfless or long-suffering.

These perceptions reinforce the pattern and delay recognition of the underlying resentment.

Meanwhile, resentment continues to express itself indirectly—through inefficiency, illness, forgetfulness, or emotional withdrawal. Because the anger is hidden, it is rarely addressed.

Passive anger creates a particular kind of relational confusion. The person appears agreeable while simultaneously resisting cooperation. Others experience frustration but cannot easily identify its source, which often leads to escalating demands or criticism—responses that further reinforce the original pattern.

The Cost of Living Behind the Smile

Over time, passive anger exacts a toll. Relationships lose vitality. Communication becomes strained. Intimacy suffers.

The individual may feel chronically tired, depressed, or unfulfilled. They may believe that life is unfair or that others are demanding too much, without recognizing their own role in sustaining the pattern.

Living behind the smile requires constant emotional labor. The effort to suppress anger consumes energy that could otherwise be used for connection, creativity, and growth.

Moving Toward Change

Change begins with recognition. Understanding that passive anger was once protective allows individuals to approach change with compassion rather than shame.

Learning to express anger directly does not mean becoming aggressive or confrontational. It means developing the capacity to notice anger early, tolerate the discomfort it brings, and communicate needs and limits clearly.

This process takes time. It involves unlearning long-held beliefs about safety, approval, and worth. It also requires practicing new skills—setting boundaries, saying no, and tolerating the anxiety that may follow.

As individuals begin to replace indirect expression with direct communication, the need for the smile diminishes. Energy once spent managing resentment becomes available for genuine connection.

The goal is not to eliminate anger, but to integrate it—allowing it to inform rather than control behavior.

Closing Reflection

Behind the smile often lies anger that was never given a voice. When that anger is finally recognized and understood, it no longer needs to hide. Passive anger is only one way anger learns to hide. In the chapters ahead we will examine other anger languages that appear very different on the surface yet serve many of the same protective functions.

CHAPTER FOUR

THE SHORT FUSE

Explosive Anger

Explosive anger is the most visible and dramatic of the anger patterns. When it erupts, it does so with speed and intensity, often overwhelming both the individual and those nearby. For people who rely on this pattern, anger is not experienced as a feeling that gradually emerges and can be reflected upon. Instead, it arrives as a force that overtakes the body and mind simultaneously.

Individuals who struggle with explosive anger often describe the experience as sudden and overpowering. Their anger erupts quickly, frequently with little warning, and escalates far beyond the circumstances that triggered it. Rather than building gradually, the reaction can move from calm to rage in seconds.

Once activated, these individuals often feel out of control, as though a switch has been flipped that cannot easily be turned off. Many describe "seeing red," "blacking out," or simply "losing it." Afterwards they may feel remorseful, ashamed, or bewildered by their own behavior. Despite sincere intentions to control their anger, the pattern repeats.

What distinguishes explosive anger is not simply intensity but lack of modulation. There is little middle ground—no meaningful space between irritation and rage.

The stories that follow illustrate this pattern in different lives and circumstances. Though the individuals differ widely in personality and background, their experience of anger is strikingly similar. Anger arrives suddenly, escalates rapidly, and is followed by regret, fear, and often significant consequences.

Same pattern. Different faces.

Barry

Barry phoned my secretary early in the week asking for an immediate appointment. Eventually he settled for the earliest available time rather than the one he wanted, which was to see me the moment he arrived.

When we met he was quiet at first, introducing himself and shaking my hand. The moment he sat down across from me, however, his composure shifted. He was a handsome man in his late forties, dressed in expensive casual clothes, smiling with the calm confidence of someone accustomed to making a good first impression.

The first thing he said was, "I'm turning fifty in three days and I can't handle it. Deep down I'm just afraid it's all catching up with me."

As the session unfolded, Barry began to describe what he meant.

When he was in eighth grade, Barry—who looked older than his years—used his appearance to get involved with alcohol and casual sex. He skipped school frequently, spending afternoons cruising around town, sneaking into movies, and eventually getting involved in petty theft. Throughout all of this he maintained a clean-cut, trustworthy image. His parents believed his explanations for the items he acquired under questionable circumstances.

At seventeen he was arrested for car theft and joyriding. Six months later, however, he completed high school and impressed the authorities with what they described as a "compliant and goal-directed attitude." They were sufficiently impressed that they not only released him but emancipated him from his parents, granting him adult status at the age of seventeen.

As an adult Barry continued to live something of a double life. He worked in sales and held a series of jobs over the years.

"I always start off well," he told me. "I jump into the job with both feet. I impress the new boss. But it never lasts."

"What happens?" I asked.

"I don't know," he replied. "I get really excited about the job at first. Then it starts to look like all the other jobs. I get sloppy. I stop caring. Eventually they ask me to leave."

"They fire you?"

"No, not exactly. They usually give me a recommendation before they let me go."

Barry told the story calmly, almost casually, as if he were describing someone else's life. Eventually I asked how any of this connected to his upcoming birthday.

"It's just that I can't keep up anymore," he said.

"You mean you can't keep changing jobs?"

"Hell no, that's no problem," he replied. "Let me explain."

Barry leaned forward and rested his head in his hands for nearly a full minute before speaking again.

"The police know me well."

"Not for crimes," he added quickly. "Not now. I gave all that up years ago. But I fight a lot."

"Do you fight often?"

"Well, I always have. When I was a kid I fought a lot. I guess it just carried over into adulthood. A lot of times it seems like I'm just in the wrong place at the wrong time."

He paused.

"I'm getting too old for that stuff. One of these days it's going to kill me."

Barry never returned after his fiftieth birthday. I often wondered what eventually caught up with him.

Greg: Always One Step Too Far

"I spent last night in jail."

Greg sat across from me looking exhausted. His expensive silk suit was wrinkled, his hair disheveled, his eyes red-rimmed and weary.

"Imagine," he said, tugging at his sleeve, "my wife didn't even bail me out until this morning."

He shook his head in disbelief.

"Why do these things keep happening? I'm a responsible, reasonable, successful adult. Everything goes along fine—up to a point. Then I just lose it."

Greg and his wife had planned an evening out at a concert by a performer he had wanted to see for years. He had paid a premium price for the tickets and was determined that nothing would interfere with the evening.

But things did interfere.

A work emergency delayed their departure. Traffic slowed them further. By the time they arrived the concert had already begun. The only parking spaces were nearly a mile away.

When they finally reached the auditorium, Greg approached an usher and asked for directions to their seats.

The usher made a sweeping gesture toward the darkened rows of the hall.

"When that happened," Greg said quietly, "I snapped."

He described feeling a surge of heat through his body. His thoughts narrowed instantly. The gesture felt dismissive, almost insulting.

Before he realized what he was doing he was shouting.

Security arrived. Police were called. Greg spent the night in jail.

By morning the anger had disappeared, replaced by disbelief and shame.

"One more sentence," he said quietly. "One more move. Always one step too far."

A Shared Pattern

Barry and Greg differ in background, temperament, and circumstance. Yet their experience of anger is remarkably similar.

Explosive anger arrives as a full-body event. The nervous system mobilizes quickly. Thought narrows. Reflection disappears.

Under stress the brain tends to follow its most familiar pathways. Like a well-worn highway, neural routes that have been used repeatedly allow for rapid response. If anger has been practiced often enough, it becomes the nervous system's fastest route.

When pressure rises, the brain does not pause to consider alternatives. It simply takes the road it knows best.

No Middle Ground

Individuals who rely on explosive anger often have little awareness of their emotional state until it has already reached an extreme level.

Mild irritation may go unnoticed. Frustration is brushed aside. Anger is not experienced as a signal that something needs attention but as a sudden eruption.

Because there is little gradual buildup, there is little opportunity to intervene early. The shift from calm to rage happens so quickly that both the individual and those around them may be caught off guard.

Once the explosion begins, it often feels unstoppable.

This pattern leaves many people feeling powerless. They may sincerely believe that anger simply happens to them—that it arrives beyond their control.

Promises to "never do it again" are often heartfelt and sincere.

And often broken.

The problem is not lack of willpower.

The problem is lack of awareness at the earliest stages of activation.

Dawn: Rage and Regret

After meeting every week for four months, Dawn and I had made little progress. Each session she wondered aloud whether therapy was helping, and each session she scheduled another appointment.

Dawn was forty years old and the mother of two children. She was strikingly attractive—a tall, willowy blonde with clear blue eyes and skin the color of honey. Her clothes were always carefully coordinated designer sportswear.

Even her personality seemed carefully selected.

She had come to therapy complaining of "depression," though her description of it was vague. She said she wasn't sleeping well and had little appetite—for either food or sex.

One afternoon she began a session by mentioning a conversation with a neighbor.

"She told me all about her childhood," Dawn said. "Awful things. I couldn't stand listening to it. Thank God the phone rang."

I asked whether hearing the story stirred anything for her.

"Actually," she replied, "I was more focused on the fact that her house needs paint. I've been interested in exterior design lately. I even went to a seminar on mixing authentic Colonial colors."

The pattern repeated week after week. Whenever conversation moved toward emotional territory, Dawn redirected it toward something neutral.

Eventually the truth emerged—not from Dawn, but from her nine-year-old son.

One morning she called to ask if she could bring Jimmy with her because his babysitter was ill. I agreed.

Jimmy wandered toward the toys in the office while Dawn and I continued talking.

As I watched him play, he began acting out a scene with two dolls and a toy car.

The small boy doll cried, "Don't go, Mommy. Don't make me go."

The mother doll shouted back, "Get in the car right now!"

Jimmy drove the car wildly across the floor, yelling as the doll screamed, "Get out of the way, you idiot!"

He stopped the car at his mother's feet and looked up.

Dawn's eyes filled with tears.

"I'm afraid to tell you," she whispered. "I'm afraid you'll leave me like everyone else."

She ran her fingers through Jimmy's hair.

"What he just did—that's me," she said quietly. "The screaming and the cursing."

Over the following weeks Dawn described sudden eruptions of anger she had experienced since childhood. Each episode had been followed by loss—friends leaving, family members distancing themselves, relationships ending.

Eventually she began driving alone whenever she felt overwhelmed.

"I'd get in the car and scream," she said. "I thought if nobody heard me it wouldn't hurt anyone."

Except Jimmy had heard.

Over time Dawn slowly learned to recognize the early sensations that preceded her outbursts and to release the pressure before it reached the breaking point.

Where Explosive Anger Begins

Explosive anger rarely appears without a history.

Many individuals who struggle with sudden outbursts grew up in environments where emotional regulation was inconsistent or poorly modeled.

In some families anger was expressed loudly and unpredictably. Children learned to remain alert, scanning for danger and preparing for the next eruption.

In other families anger was suppressed or punished. Frustration was ridiculed or ignored. Children learned to hide early feelings until the pressure became unbearable.

In both situations children were never taught how to recognize anger early and respond to it constructively.

Instead anger was experienced only at the extremes—either forbidden or overwhelming.

Over time the nervous system adapts. Subtle emotional signals are missed. The body moves quickly from calm to high arousal.

By adulthood the reaction feels automatic.

Cultural Reinforcement

Explosive anger is also reinforced by culture.

A society that rewards speed, dominance, and emotional intensity encourages immediate reaction rather than reflection. Media and social platforms amplify outrage and reward dramatic responses.

In such an environment explosive anger may appear powerful, even when it carries enormous personal cost.

Andy

Andy came to therapy at the request of his employer after a workplace confrontation that nearly became physical.

"I didn't hit him," Andy said quickly. "I could have, but I didn't."

Andy was in his late twenties, physically imposing and restless. He leaned forward in his chair, hands clasped tightly together.

"They act like I'm dangerous," he said. "I'm not dangerous. I just don't let people walk all over me."

He described feeling a sudden surge of anger whenever he believed someone was disrespecting him.

"It's like a switch flips," he explained. "Once it happens, there's no stopping it."

Growing up, Andy had lived in a household where anger was common and arguments escalated quickly.

"If you backed down, you lost," he said. "That's just how it was."

Over time anger became his primary form of self-protection.

It worked—at least in the short term.

But the cost was high.

Friendships faded. Romantic relationships ended. Career opportunities began to disappear.

"I don't want to end up alone or locked up," he admitted quietly. "I just don't know how to stop."

Interrupting the Pattern

For individuals accustomed to explosive anger, slowing down can feel unnatural—even threatening. Yet interruption is possible.

The key is recognizing the earliest physical signals of activation.

These signals often include tightening muscles, faster breathing, rising body heat, agitation, or an urgent need to act.

When these cues are noticed early enough, even a brief pause can interrupt the escalation.

Building Distress Tolerance

The ability to interrupt anger during conflict depends largely on what has been practiced outside those moments.

Practices such as meditation, controlled breathing, mindful walking, yoga, or tai chi expose the nervous system to slower rhythms of awareness.

These practices do not eliminate anger. Instead they increase the capacity to remain present with emotional intensity without immediately acting on it.

With repetition, the brain learns that strong emotions can be experienced without catastrophe.

New pathways develop.

Awareness arrives earlier.

Choice becomes possible.

Reclaiming Assertive Rights

As regulation improves, many individuals discover that anger had been expressing needs that were never spoken directly.

Assertiveness is not about domination. It is about reclaiming the right to express oneself clearly and respectfully.

Basic Assertive Rights include:

- The right to say no
- The right to express feelings without aggression
- The right to ask for what you need
- The right to change your mind
- The right to make mistakes
- The right to set limits
- The right to be treated with respect
- The right to pause before responding
- The right to care for yourself without abandoning others

Reflection as Practice

Learning from anger requires reflection.

Questions that support this process include:

- What am I feeling beneath my impulse to react?
- What does this situation remind me of?

- What am I trying to protect through anger?
- What boundary may be crossed or unspoken?
- What response would reflect the person I want to become?

Used consistently, these questions help translate emotional activation into understanding and choice. They reinforce the shift from reaction to reflection, from performance to presence, and from anger as a driver to anger as information.

Closing Reflection

Explosive anger is not a failure of character.

It is a learned response to threat, shaped by experience and reinforced through repetition.

Though the individuals differ, the pattern remains recognizable. And patterns, once understood, can change.

Yet explosive anger is only one form anger takes.

Sometimes anger does not explode in the moment. Instead it waits quietly, gathering strength and searching for a way to balance the scales.

Rather than erupting, it calculates.

The next chapter explores this quieter but equally powerful pattern—the anger that says

"You'll Get Yours."

CHAPTER FIVE

Retaliatory Anger

Retaliatory anger differs fundamentally from explosive anger. Where explosive anger erupts in the heat of the moment, retaliatory anger is held in reserve—calculated rather than immediate, organized around timing rather than discharge. Grievances are remembered, stored, and revisited. Slights are magnified. Intentions are assumed. Motives are questioned.

Retaliatory anger is fueled by the belief that harm must be answered with harm. Justice becomes personal. Forgiveness is equated with weakness. To let go of a grievance feels dangerous, as though it invites further injury. Relief does not come through expression, but through restoration of power. Waiting becomes part of the strategy. Patience is not peace; it is preparation.

This pattern often appears controlled on the surface. There may be long periods of apparent calm. But the calm is deceptive. Anger is being organized, not resolved.

The Logic of Retaliation

Unlike the eruption of explosive anger in the heat of the moment, retaliatory anger is held in reserve. It is calculated rather than immediate, organized around timing rather than discharge. Grievances are remembered, stored, and revisited. Slights are magnified, intentions assumed, and motives questioned.

Retaliatory anger is fueled by a belief that harm must be answered with harm. Justice becomes personal. Forgiveness is equated with weakness. To let go of a grievance feels dangerous, as though it invites further injury.

Relief does not come through expression, but through restoration of power. Waiting becomes part of the strategy. Patience is not peace; it is preparation.

This form of anger often appears controlled, even reasonable. There may be long periods of apparent calm. But the calm is deceptive. Anger is being organized, not resolved.

Testing the World

For individuals who rely on retaliatory anger, the world is not entered freely; it is tested. Trust is provisional. Safety is conditional. Others are approached with caution rather than openness, not because connection is unwanted, but because harm is expected.

Early experiences taught these individuals that injury often went unacknowledged and that vulnerability carried risk. Appeals for fairness or care were unreliable. As a result, anger became organized not around expression, but around anticipation. Retaliation developed as a way to manage uncertainty: If I stay vigilant, I will not be surprised.

Testing the world is not always overt. It may take the form of withholding information, delaying response, or setting up situations that reveal how others will behave under strain. When people fail these tests, anger is justified. When they pass, the testing often continues, because safety never feels fully secure.

In this way, retaliatory anger functions less as a reaction to what has happened and more as a strategy for confirming what is believed to be true; that harm is inevitable and must be met with strength rather than openness. Children who develop this pattern often begin testing the world long before they have the language to describe what they are doing.

Jason's life illustrates this process in its earliest and most stark form.

Jason

Jason was eleven when he came to my office on a trial visit with John and Carol, the couple who were going to adopt him. He was a small, frail boy with dark hair, dark eyes, and a dark complexion. His crooked, broken boxer's nose also spoke of a dark past. He had been in a number of street fights and had been placed in several foster homes over the years.

When they arrived at my office, Jason bolted into the room before anyone else and commandeered my desk chair, spinning it around and straddling it backwards.

"I bet you're gonna want to know all about my family and that sorta junk," he said, his feet dangling off the chair. "I've been through this before and it's no big deal. I'm ready for ya, so go ahead."

Before I could respond, Jason interrupted again.

"All that stuff's over now," he said. "You can ask me anything 'cause everything's gonna be different now." He nodded sheepishly toward John and Carol. "They're gonna be my parents. I got a brand-new family."

Having a family was a new experience for Jason. At his birth, his biological mother was sixteen years old and using drugs, and his father was forty-five, a gambler and a transient. Jason spent his first four years living with various relatives before he was placed in foster care, where again he was passed from home to home.

As Jason talked, it became clear that he had learned early how to charm adults. He knew what to say, when to say it, and how to say it in a way that put others at ease. His confidence was striking, particularly given how little stability he had known.

John and Carol listened quietly, hopeful and eager to believe this adoption would succeed. Jason, for his part, seemed determined to present himself as cooperative and untroubled.

Shortly after the placement, Jason left the window open behind him at night. The cat he had adopted crawled along a ledge and scratched at John and Carol's bedroom window. This alerted them that Jason was gone. John searched the neighborhood and eventually found Jason playing video games at a local bowling alley.

Two days later, the cat was found dead, strangled under the backyard fence.

Jason denied responsibility, and John and Carol, horrified by the act, were only too ready to forget it. But the cat was only the beginning. Money began to disappear. Clothing was shredded. Flowers were trampled. Furniture was broken. Jason denied knowing anything about the damage, but John and Carol no longer believed him.

The final incident occurred when Jason set fire to the garage while they were away.

A year and a half after Jason arrived, he was returned to county care. By thirteen, he was placed in a group home. Soon after, he ran away, broke into John and Carol's house, and stole two shotguns. He was caught that night hiding nearby with the guns.

Jason spent the next five years in juvenile detention.

Understanding Jason

Jason's behavior was not random, nor was it senseless cruelty. It was organized around one central question: When will love fail?

Each act tested the durability of attachment. Each escalation asked whether care would remain when innocence was stripped away. Retaliation functioned as both shield and probe—a way to protect against surprise and to confirm long-held expectations about abandonment.

Jason did not trust repair because repair had never been reliable. Testing replaced trust. Retaliation replaced appeal. Most individuals who organize anger this way never set fires or steal guns.

Yet the psychological structure behind Jason's behavior often persists in quieter forms. The testing becomes more subtle, the retaliation more socially acceptable, but the underlying questions remains the same: Can people be trusted not to harm or abandon me?

Adult Expressions of Retaliatory Anger

In adulthood, retaliatory anger becomes more socially acceptable and more difficult to recognize. It may take the form of emotional withdrawal, delayed confrontation, silent treatment, or calculated remarks delivered long after the original offense.

Because expression is delayed, others often experience these moments as sudden or disproportionate. The individual, however, experiences them as justified and restrained.

"I waited."

"I gave them time."

"They needed to understand."

The anger feels measured, controlled, and morally sound. What is less visible is how long it has been rehearsed internally. In relationships, this may appear as bringin up a grievance months after it occurred, presenting it not as a complaint but as a verdict. In workplaces, it may appear as quiet sabotage – waiting for the right moment to undermine someone who caused embarrassment. Within families, it may emerge as a long memory for slights, resurfacing during moments of conflict long after others assumed the issue had been resolved.

Fairness as a Worldview

A central organizing principle for those with this pattern is fairness. Life is evaluated through the lens of justice, balance, and equity.

When fairness is violated, anger is triggered. When injury goes unrecognized, resentment grows. Retaliation restores balance—not emotionally, but morally.

This worldview provides structure and certainty. It also narrows possibility. Conversations become verdicts. Conflicts become trials. Repair becomes difficult once judgment has been rendered.

Jim's life illustrates how fairness can become a lens through which all relationships are evaluated.

Jim

Jim came to therapy at the insistence of his wife. He believed he was reasonable, controlled, and fair. Anger, in his view, was something others lacked discipline around.

"I don't get angry easily," he said. "But when I do, I don't forget."

Jim grew up in a household where mistakes were costly and apologies rarely erased consequences. Once you were in trouble, you stayed there. As an adult, Jim prided himself on patience. When wronged, he withdrew rather than reacted. He waited.

"I don't lose my temper," he said. "I just let people understand what they've done."

His wife experienced this as devastating. By the time Jim spoke, his words landed as verdicts rather than conversations. For Jim, retaliation was protection. Letting go felt like surrender.

Conditional Love and the Ledger of Injury

Many individuals who rely on retaliatory anger grew up in environments where love felt conditional and easily withdrawn. Approval was earned through behavior, compliance, or vigilance.

In such contexts, keeping track becomes essential. The ledger of injury ensures that harm is not erased or denied. Memory becomes protection.

This internal ledger persists into adulthood. Slights are recorded, intentions questioned, and grievances stored for later use. Retaliation becomes the means by which balance is restored and self-respect preserved.

Alexis's life reveals how conditional love shapes adult relationships organized around retaliation rather than trust.

Alexis

Alexis came to therapy following the end of a long relationship. She described herself as someone who consistently gave more than she received and paid the price for it. She tolerated disappointments quietly, keeping track of what she felt she could not say.

"When I finally speak," she said, "it's already too late."

Her anger emerged as carefully constructed confrontations, calm in tone and overwhelming in content. Alexis grew up in an environment where love felt conditional and easily withdrawn. Keeping score became a way to ensure that injury was not erased or denied. By the time anger surfaced, the relationship was already closing.

Early Roots of Retaliatory Anger

From a developmental perspective, retaliatory anger often emerges in response to repeated experiences of unfairness, inconsistency, or emotional neglect.

When caregivers fail to acknowledge harm or respond reliably, children learn that direct appeal is ineffective. They adapt by becoming watchful, self-protective, and internally organized around justice rather than connection.

Over time, this stance becomes embodied. Anger is not felt as an emotion to be expressed, but as a resource to be deployed when needed.

Internal Working Model and Self-Fulfillment

An internal working model takes shape: If I do not remember, I will be hurt again.

If I do not remember, I will be hurt again. If I forgive too easily, I will be taken advantage of. If I stay vigilant, I remain safe.

This model becomes self-fulfilling. Retaliation confirms expectations about others while limiting opportunities for repair. Relationships end not in chaos, but in quiet certainty.

The individual feels justified—and alone.

Corrine's life illustrates how this internal model becomes both protection and prison.

Corrine

Corrine described herself as someone who learned early not to rely on others. She remembered everything.

"I don't forget," she said. "That's how I protect myself."

Her anger was deliberate. She waited, watched, and confronted with precision.

"I don't explode," she said. "I decide."

Friends experienced Corrine as controlled and formidable. Disagreements rarely turned into arguments, but they often ended relationships. By the time Corrine spoke, the outcome had already been determined.

Corrine's retaliation restored control but foreclosed repair. Relationships ended quietly, and without reconciliation.

Why Retaliation Feels Necessary

Simply stated, retaliation restores balance.

It protects against helplessness. It ensures that injury is acknowledged. It reasserts control when vulnerability feels unsafe. For many people, the moment of retaliation brings a powerful sense of moral clarity. The score has been evened. The harm has been recognized. The imbalance has been corrected. What follows, however, is rarely the connection that was hoped for. Retaliation may restore dignity, but it rarely restores intimacy.

The protection it provides comes at a cost; the gradual narrowing of relationships and the quiet reinforcement of the belief that others cannot be trusted.

Toward Change

Change begins with recognizing that retaliatory anger was once adaptive. It served a protective function in environments where safety and fairness were uncertain.

Moving beyond this pattern requires learning to speak earlier, tolerate discomfort, and risk repair. It involves loosening the grip on the ledger and developing trust—not blind trust, but earned trust.

Letting go does not mean forgetting. It means choosing not to live bound to past injury.

Closing Reflection

Retaliatory anger is not about cruelty. It is about survival. When its purpose is understood, it no longer has to dictate the future. Some individuals retaliate directly. Others pursue a different strategy – one that does not attack openly but binds others through obligation, guilt, and moral pressure.

That form of anger is quieter, but no less powerful.

CHAPTER SIX

YOU'RE KILLING YOUR FATHER

Guilt Inducing Anger

Anger does not always speak the same language.

Sometimes it explodes in confrontation. Sometimes it retreats into silence. Sometimes it turns inward as shame.

And sometimes anger speaks through guilt.

In this language, suffering becomes the message. Emotional pain signals that someone else has done something wrong. Others feel compelled to repair the distress even when the anger behind it has never been spoken directly.

This chapter explores the anger language of guilt—how it develops, how it operates within relationships, and why it is so powerful.

Renee said loudly to her parents, "It's not me who's going to end up killing Dad. It's you—for forcing me to do the stupid things you want."

Her mother froze.

"Renee," she said, shaken, "you're the one who's killing your father."

Renee's father had a long history of heart problems, and her mother lived in constant fear that one of Renee's emotional episodes might trigger a medical crisis. The argument stopped immediately.

Moments like this can appear dramatic, manipulative, or irrational. But scenes like this are rarely random. They reflect a particular way anger learns to communicate when direct protest feels unsafe.

In this pattern anger is not expressed through confrontation. Instead it appears as suffering. Emotional distress becomes evidence that someone else has done something wrong. Others are made responsible not only for the person's feelings, but for their stability, safety, or well-being.

In the language of anger, guilt becomes the translation. For many people this pattern develops long before they have words for it. Direct anger may have discouraged, punished, or ignored in early relationships. Expressions of frustration might have been labeled disrespectful, selfish, or hurtful. In such environments the child learns that open protest carries risk. But emotional suffering is harder to dismiss.

When distress is visible – tears, despair, withdrawal – others often respond quickly. Concern replaces criticism. Protection replaces discipline. Over time, the nervous system learns an important lesson: pain gains response when anger cannot. Without conscious intention, anger begins to travel through suffering.

Renee

Renee was fifteen when her parents brought her to therapy. She did not come willingly. She entered the office several steps ahead of them, dropped heavily into the chair farthest from the door, and stared at the floor. Her arms were folded tightly across her chest. When I spoke to her, she did not answer. When her parents began explaining why they were there, she interrupted them.

"You don't have to explain," she said flatly. "I already know. I'm the problem."

Her mother looked stricken. Her father leaned forward in his chair, hands clasped together, as if bracing himself.

Renee had been having frequent emotional outbursts at home—crying spells, accusations, dramatic statements about how no one cared about her. At school she alternated between charm and hostility. Teachers described her as intelligent but volatile.

As the session progressed, something became clear. When Renee became upset, everything stopped. Arguments ended. Decisions were reconsidered. Plans were abandoned. Her parents shifted immediately into crisis management, trying to calm her distress.

Renee had noticed this. When I asked what usually happened at home when she became upset, she shrugged.

"They freak out," she said. "They'll do anything to get me to calm down."

Her emotions escalated quickly and dramatically. If she felt ignored, she became overwhelmed. If she felt disappointed, she collapsed into tears. If she felt angry, her words became accusatory.

The intensity of her feelings created urgency. Her parents responded not to what she said, but to how badly she seemed to feel.

Renee was discovering something powerful: emotional suffering was the most reliable way to be heard.

During one session her mother described a recent argument about curfew. Renee had wanted to stay out later than agreed upon. When her parents refused, the situation escalated quickly.

The argument ended the moment her distress intensified. Curfew was no longer the issue. Her parents were focused entirely on calming her down. Whether she understood it consciously or not, Renee was learning something important: When her pain became urgent enough, everything else stopped. Intensity brought response. Ordinary frustration did not.

As we explored earlier experiences, a pattern emerged. Renee had grown up in a household where emotions were taken very seriously—but boundaries were not. Her parents were deeply invested in protecting her from distress. When she was upset, they rushed to fix the problem, often abandoning limits in the process.

Renee learned that intensity worked. By adolescence her emotional reactions had become both genuine and instrumental. She experienced them fully, but she had also learned to rely on them. Emotional collapse—and later emotional threat—became a way of controlling outcomes.

Beneath her accusations was something else entirely.

Fear.

During one session, when the room had been quiet for some time, she spoke softly.

"I don't want to hurt them," she said. "I just can't stand it when they don't take me seriously."

Being heard had come to require a crisis.

It is important to understand that emotions expressed this way are not necessarily fabricated. Renee's distress was real. What had developed over time was a system in which emotional intensity served two purposes simultaneously. It reflected her genuine feelings, and it also influenced the behavior of those around her.

This dual function can be confusing both for the individual and for those who love them. Parents may wonder whether the suffering is authentic or manipulative. The person experiencing it may feel ashamed or misunderstood, sensing that others doubt their sincerity. In reality the pattern reflects learning rather than deception. The nervous system has discovered a reliable method of securing attention and protection.

When Distress Becomes a Language

Adolescence is often where this pattern becomes visible.Children who grow up in emotionally reactive environments learn quickly what kinds of expression produce response. Calm protest may be ignored. Ordinary frustration may be dismissed. But emotional crisis commands attention.

Without anyone intending it, the family system begins to reward intensity.

The child does not set out to manipulate. She discovers a language that works.

Suffering produces response. Distress brings protection. Emotional urgency reorganizes the room. Over time the nervous system learns that ordinary anger is not enough. To be heard, it must escalate.

Renee's story illustrates a pattern that appears in many different forms. When anger cannot be expressed directly, it often finds another route—one that makes others responsible for the distress it creates.

To understand why this pattern is so powerful, it helps to understand the role guilt plays in regulating human behavior.

Why Guilt Works

Guilt is one of the most powerful regulators of human behavior. Unlike anger or fear, which may provoke resistance, guilt compels repair. When someone believes they have caused harm, the impulse to correct the damage is immediate.

In guilt-inducing anger emotional distress becomes evidence that someone else has done something wrong. The message is rarely stated outright, but it is unmistakable: If I am suffering, someone must be responsible.

Those around the individual begin organizing their behavior around preventing the next accusation. Decisions are shaped not by personal judgment, but by the desire to avoid causing harm.

Compliance becomes the safest option. It resolves the immediate tension, even if the underlying conflict remains untouched. Over time the relationship reorganizes itself around emotional pressure rather than open negotiation. Guilt is particularly powerful because it operates internally. Unlike anger, which invites confrontation, guilt reorganizes behavior from within. The person who believes they have caused harms begins regulating themselves in order to repair the perceived injury.

They apologize. They adjust their behavior. They become cautious about future actions. For the person expressing distress, this shift can feel like relief. The emotional pressure has succeeded in restoring connection or influence. Yet the underlying issue often remains unspoken. The conflict that produced the distress is replaced by a cycle of injury and repair that repeats over time.

Recognizing Guilt-Inducing Anger

Guilt-inducing anger often operates subtly. It may not look like anger at all. Instead, it appears as distress, accusation, or emotional suffering that others feel compelled to repair.

Common signs include:

- Emotional distress escalates when limits are set
- Someone's suffering is framed as evidence that another person has caused harm

- Others feel responsible for preventing the person's upset
- Boundaries are experienced as cruelty or abandonment
- Conflicts resolve only when someone apologizes or retreats
- The person expressing distress does not experience themselves as angry, only hurt or misunderstood

In these situations, anger is present, but it travels through guilt rather than direct expression.

Guilt as Control

Renee's story reveals a central feature of guilt-inducing anger: control achieved through emotional suffering rather than direct assertion. Anger is expressed as injury. Distress becomes proof of wrongdoing. Others feel compelled to repair the situation, even when they are unsure what they have done wrong. This pattern is rarely experienced as manipulative by the person expressing it. The feelings are real.

What often goes unrecognized is how emotional intensity creates urgency—how suffering becomes a demand rather than a signal. When anger operates this way, resistance feels cruel. Boundaries feel like abandonment. Compliance becomes the path of least harm.Over time this dynamic reshapes relationships and quietly redistributes power.

Erosion of Self-Trust

Those on the receiving end of guilt-inducing anger often begin to doubt themselves. Perceptions are questioned. Intentions are scrutinized. Emotional reactions become filtered through self-blame. The question gradually shifts from:

What am I feeling?

to

What have I done wrong?

As self-trust erodes, responsibility expands. Anger is absorbed rather than expressed, setting the stage for complementary patterns to emerge within intimate relationships.

Ellen and Jasper illustrate how guilt-inducing anger and guilt-absorbing anger can become entwined.

Ellen and Jasper

Ellen and Jasper came to therapy after years of what they described as communication problems. They sat close together on the couch but seemed strangely disconnected.

Ellen spoke first.

"We just can't seem to talk without it turning into something," she said. "I say one thing and he hears another."

Jasper nodded quickly.

"I try not to upset her," he added. "That's usually when things go wrong."

As the sessions unfolded, a familiar pattern emerged.

Ellen experienced Jasper as emotionally absent and inattentive. Jasper experienced Ellen as overwhelming and unpredictable.

When Ellen felt unheard, her distress escalated quickly.

"You don't care," she would say. "If you cared, you wouldn't do this to me."

Jasper responded by trying harder to soothe her.

"I didn't mean it that way," he said. "I'll fix it. Just tell me what you need."

These moments often ended with Jasper apologizing or changing his behavior. Ellen calmed. The immediate tension subsided. But nothing was resolved.

In one session Ellen described an argument from the previous week. Jasper had forgotten to call when he was running late.

"I was sick with worry," she said. "I thought something terrible had happened."

Jasper looked helpless.

"I didn't think it was a big deal," he said. "I just got stuck at work."

Ellen turned toward him.

"You know how anxious I get," she said. "How could you do that to me?"

Jasper nodded quietly.

"I should have known better."

As he spoke, responsibility shifted almost invisibly. Jasper's behavior was framed not as a mistake but as an injury. Ellen's anxiety became evidence of wrongdoing.

When I asked Jasper what happened to his own anger in moments like these, he seemed confused.

"I don't really get angry," he said. "I just try to make it right."

Each was regulating the other's anxiety without recognizing it.

Their conflict was not about communication. It was about how anger had been learned, expressed, and managed in relationship. Couples caught in this dynamic often describe their relationship as loving but exhausting. Both partners are attempting to preserve connection, yet they do so through incompatible strategies. The partner expressing distress feels unseen and escalates emotion in order o secure reassurance. The partner absorbing guilt attempts to restore calm by accepting responsibility and minimizing conflict. Neither strategy resolves the underlying tension. One partner never feels fully heard. The other never feels fully free. Over time, both begin to experience resentment, even while insisting that the relationship itself is important.

The Cost of Guilt-Inducing Anger

While guilt-inducing anger may preserve connection in the short term, its long-term cost is profound. Relationships become organized around obligation rather than choice. Love becomes entangled with responsibility. Autonomy begins to feel like betrayal.

Those who induce guilt often feel powerless to ask directly for what they need. Those who absorb guilt feel responsible for emotions they cannot control.

Resentment accumulates on both sides.

Neither person feels free.

Toward Change

Change begins with recognition. For those who rely on guilt as a regulatory strategy, growth requires tolerating the direct expression of anger—learning to say what hurts or disappoints without escalating into accusation or collapse. For those who absorb guilt, change involves recognizing where responsibility ends and boundaries begin. In both cases the work is uncomfortable. It challenges long-held beliefs about worth, duty, and love.

But as these patterns shift, relationships begin to reorganize around choice rather than emotional pressure. Recognizing guilt-inducing anger can be uncomfortable for everyone involved. Those who rely on it may fear being seen as manipulative or unfair. Those who absorb it may worry that setting limits will appear cold or uncaring. In reality the pattern reflects a relational system that developed gradually. Each participant adapted in ways that once helped preserve connection. What no appears dysfunctional may have once felt necessary. Understanding the pattern allows both individuals to step out of the roles they have been unconsciously playing.

Closing Reflection

Guilt is one of the most powerful forces in human relationships. It binds people together, organizes behavior, and compels repair. When anger learns to travel through guilt, connection may appear preserved. But the relationship slowly reorganizes around emotional pressure rather than honest expression.

One person suffers. The other rushes to fix. Anger moves through the system, but it is rarely spoken directly. Understanding this pattern does not assign blame. It restores clarity. What once looked like manipulation often began as adaptation—a way of protecting connection when anger felt dangerous.

But adaptation has consequences. When anger can finally be spoken plainly, guilt no longer needs to carry its message. Responsibility can return to its rightful place, and relationships can reorganize around choice rather than emotional obligation.

Guilt-inducing anger rarely exists alone. It often finds its counterpart in someone willing to absorb responsibility for emotional distress. One person escalates suffering. The other works to repair it. If this chapter explored the language of guilt used outwardly—making others responsible for emotional pain—the next examines the opposite pattern: anger that turns inward, where responsibility expands and protest disappears.

This is the pattern of guilt-absorbing anger.

CHAPTER SEVEN

YOU'RE PROBABLY RIGHT

Guilt-Absorbing Anger

Anger Turned Inward

Not all anger is expressed outwardly. Some anger is turned inward, absorbed, and carried as guilt, responsibility, and self-doubt. In this pattern, anger is not denied—but it is redirected. Rather than being expressed toward those who provoke it, anger is folded back onto the self.

Individuals who organize around guilt absorption often believe that conflict threatens connection. Anger, especially their own, feels dangerous. It risks rejection, abandonment, or emotional chaos. As a result, anger is managed by assuming blame, minimizing needs, and maintaining harmony at personal cost.

This pattern is frequently rooted in early experiences of parentification—situations in which a child learned that caring for others was necessary for safety or belonging. Emotional responsibility came too early, and anger had nowhere to go.

Over time, anger became guilt.

Carol

Carol came to therapy at the insistence of her husband, though she insisted that she was "probably the problem."

She sat across from me with a tentative smile, speaking carefully, as if every word needed to be measured before it was allowed out.

"I know I'm sensitive," she said. "I probably overreact."

Carol described a marriage in which disagreements were subtle but persistent. When her husband was dissatisfied, he became distant. He didn't yell or accuse. He withdrew. Carol responded by searching herself for fault.

"I replay everything," she said. "What I said. What I didn't say. What I should have known."

When I asked how she felt toward her husband when he was dismissive or critical, she paused.

"I don't get angry," she said slowly. "I just feel bad."

Yet Carol's body told a different story. She struggled with chronic anxiety, insomnia, and a constant sense of tension. She described feeling responsible not only for her husband's moods, but for the emotional climate of the entire household.

"If something's wrong," she said, "I assume it's me."

As we talked, it became clear that Carol had learned this stance early. Growing up, she had been the emotional caretaker in her family. When her parents were overwhelmed or distressed, Carol stepped in—soothing, anticipating, managing.

There was little room for her own anger. Expressions of frustration were met with guilt.

"You're upsetting your mother."

"Your father's had a hard day."

Carol learned that harmony depended on her restraint. Anger became synonymous with harm. Turning it inward felt safer than risking disconnection.

In adulthood, this strategy preserved relationships—but eroded her sense of self. Carol doubted her perceptions, minimized her needs, and absorbed anger as guilt. What looked like kindness was, in fact, self-erasure.

From Self-Blame to Burden

Carol's story illustrates the core of the guilt-absorbing anger pattern: anger does not disappear—it is reassigned. Responsibility replaces protest. Guilt stands in for rage.

For many individuals like Carol, this pattern begins not with choice, but with necessity. When caring for others becomes essential to safety, anger must be swallowed. Over time, swallowing becomes habit.

Carol is not alone.

Other lives reveal the same pattern expressed through different circumstances—marriage, caregiving, work, and illness. In each, anger is absorbed in service of connection.

It is to these lives that we now turn.

Parentification and the Burden of Care

Parentification occurs when a child assumes emotional or practical responsibilities that belong to adults. The child becomes attuned to others 'needs while learning to ignore or suppress their own. Over time, caregiving shifts from behavior to identity.

For children who grow up in households marked by instability, illness, addiction, or emotional fragility, caring for others often feels necessary for survival. Anger, in these environments, is not tolerated. It threatens already strained systems. The child learns instead to anticipate, soothe, and accommodate.

Responsibility replaces protest.

As adults, these individuals often continue to organize relationships around care-taking. They absorb anger not because they lack it, but because expressing it feels unsafe. Guilt becomes the price of connection.

Sylvia's life illustrates how this burden is carried quietly—and for decades.

Sylvia

Sylvia described herself as "easygoing" and "low maintenance." She smiled often as she spoke, minimizing the seriousness of her concerns.

"I don't like drama," she said. "I just let things go."

Sylvia had been married for over thirty years. Her husband was demanding and critical, though not overtly cruel. When he was displeased, he became distant and cold. Sylvia responded by trying harder.

"If he's upset," she said, "I assume I've done something wrong."

When asked whether she ever felt angry with him, Sylvia looked genuinely confused.

"I don't really get angry," she said. "I just feel bad."

Sylvia grew up in a household where emotional stability depended on her vigilance. Her mother was frequently overwhelmed. Her father was withdrawn. Sylvia learned early to monitor the emotional climate, anticipating needs before they were voiced.

If someone was upset, Sylvia felt responsible. Anger had no place. Expressions of frustration were met with guilt.

"Don't make things worse."

"You know how fragile she is."

As an adult, Sylvia's anger was absorbed and redirected inward. She apologized reflexively. She questioned her perceptions. Over time, her confidence eroded.

"I don't trust myself," she said quietly. "I always think I'm missing something."

Sylvia's compliance preserved her marriage, but at significant personal cost. She felt increasingly invisible. Depression settled in—not as sadness, but as exhaustion.

Her anger was still present. It lived in self-doubt, withdrawal, and quiet resentment.

Recognizing Parentification

Sylvia did not experience herself as burdened. Caretaking felt normal. Familiar. Necessary. This is one of the most insidious aspects of parentification: it rarely feels like harm. It feels like responsibility.

Individuals who have been parentified often struggle to identify anger because it has long been intertwined with guilt and duty. Saying no feels selfish. Asserting needs feels dangerous. Sylvia's story prepares us to see how this pattern develops—and why it persists.

How Parentification Develops

Parentification often begins quietly. It does not announce itself as harm. Instead, it emerges in families where emotional or practical demands exceed what adults are able to manage. Children step in not because they are asked to, but because someone must.

In some families, illness or mental health struggles shift responsibility downward. In others, emotional immaturity, chronic stress, or unresolved trauma leaves children sensing that their own needs are burdensome. The child learns to stay alert—to notice tone, mood, and shifts in energy.

Anger, in these environments, is dangerous. It disrupts already fragile systems. The child learns that expressing frustration or protest risks loss of connection or stability. Caretaking becomes the safer choice. Over time, the child's internal working model forms around a central belief: my role is to manage others, not myself. Anger is not eliminated—it is absorbed and carried as guilt.

Laura's life shows how this early role can shape identity well into adulthood.

Laura

Laura came to therapy after her supervisor suggested she needed to be "more assertive." The comment left her embarrassed and confused.

"I don't even know what that means," she said. "I just try not to make mistakes."

Laura was in her early thirties, neatly dressed, meticulous in her speech. She apologized often—sometimes mid-sentence—without clear reason.

"I'm probably overthinking this," she said repeatedly.

Laura described growing up as the oldest child in a family where emotional needs were unevenly distributed. Her mother struggled with depression. Her father worked long hours and was largely unavailable. Laura learned early to be "the responsible one."

"If something went wrong," she said, "I felt like it was my job to fix it."

Laura became skilled at anticipating needs. She noticed shifts in mood quickly. She adjusted herself accordingly. Praise came when she was helpful. Disappointment followed when she asserted herself.

Anger was not tolerated. The internalized voice in her mind sounded like the following:

"You're being selfish."

"Why are you making this harder?"

As an adult, Laura held herself to impossible standards. When others were dissatisfied, she assumed fault.

"I should have known better," she said. "I should have tried harder." Her anger surfaced as relentless self-criticism. She worked longer hours, took on extra responsibility, and apologized preemptively. Resentment accumulated quietly, but never found expression. Laura struggled with trust—not of others, but of herself.

"I don't know when I'm allowed to be upset," she said softly. "I don't know when it's okay to say no."

Her anger had been absorbed so completely that it no longer felt like anger at all. It felt like inadequacy.

Why This Matters

Laura's story illustrates the long-term cost of parentification. When anger is absorbed rather than expressed, self-trust erodes. Individuals lose confidence in their perceptions, their needs, and their right to take up space.

Anger, when turned inward, becomes self-attack. Over time, the individual becomes both caretaker and critic, responsible for everyone's well-being while feeling perpetually at fault.

This loss of self-trust is not a character flaw. It is the residue of early responsibility carried too long.

The Cost of Guilt Absorption

Absorbing anger preserves connection, but it exacts a cumulative cost. Over time, individuals organized around guilt absorption experience a steady erosion of self-trust. Decisions become fraught. Perceptions are doubted. Needs feel illegitimate.

Because anger is redirected inward, it often appears as anxiety, depression, chronic self-criticism, or emotional numbness. The individual learns to scan for what others want while losing touch with what they themselves feel. Responsibility expands while agency contracts.

What once served as a survival strategy becomes a quiet form of self-abandonment. Anger is not resolved; it is carried—often for decades.

Bob's life illustrates how this cost accrues over time.

Bob

Bob was a quiet man in his early sixties who described himself as "easygoing" and "non-confrontational." He spoke slowly, choosing his words with care, as if trying not to disturb the space around him.

"I've always been the peacemaker," he said. "Someone has to keep things calm."

Bob grew up in a household where anger was volatile and unpredictable. When conflict erupted, it filled the house. As a child, Bob learned that staying quiet and agreeable kept him safe.

"If I stayed out of the way, things didn't get worse," he said.

Bob carried this strategy into adulthood. He avoided conflict in relationships, at work, and with friends. When disagreements arose, he assumed responsibility.

"If something's wrong," he said, "I figure it's probably me."

Bob rarely expressed anger outwardly. Instead, he withdrew. He became emotionally distant, disengaging when situations felt tense. Over time, this withdrawal hardened into numbness.

"I don't really feel much anymore," he said. "It's easier that way."

Bob's anger had not disappeared. It had been absorbed and silenced. The cost was a diminished sense of vitality and connection. He felt invisible, but safe enough to endure.

Why This Matters

Bob's story brings into focus what guilt absorption ultimately costs: a life lived cautiously, with muted emotion and constrained choice. Anger, when turned inward, does not protect indefinitely. It narrows possibility. For individuals like Bob, reclaiming anger does not mean becoming confrontational. It means allowing themselves to register displeasure, assert preferences, and tolerate the discomfort that comes with self-definition.

Without this reclamation, the pattern persists—reinforced by cultural messages that reward self-sacrifice and emotional restraint.

Do You Find Yourself Saying Things Like…

People who have learned to manage anger by absorbing it often share a familiar inner language. These phrases tend to surface during moments of tension, disappointment, or self-doubt—sometimes spoken aloud, sometimes only internally.

As you read, notice what feels familiar. There is no need to analyze or explain. Recognition alone is enough.

- "It's probably my fault."
- "I don't want to make things worse."
- "I should have handled that better."
- "It's not worth bringing up."
- "I'm probably overreacting."
- "I don't want to upset anyone."
- "Other people have it harder than I do."
- "I can deal with it."
- "I just need to try harder."
- "I don't want to be selfish."

Cultural Amplification of External Cues

For individuals organized around guilt-absorbing anger, cultural forces often intensify an already fragile relationship with self-trust. Many contemporary messages emphasize responsiveness, likability, productivity, and emotional accommodation. Being "good," "understanding," and "low maintenance" is frequently praised, while anger—especially quiet or relational anger—remains poorly tolerated.

Social media, self-help narratives, and workplace norms often reward external attunement over internal awareness. Approval becomes visible and measurable; inner signals remain vague and uncertain. For those already conditioned to monitor others closely, these external cues can further displace attention from internal experience.

Over time, the individual learns to look outward for confirmation—likes, reassurance, affirmation—while doubting internal signals of discomfort or anger. The question becomes not What do I feel? but How am I being perceived?

In this way, culture does not create guilt absorption, but it reinforces it—making self-silencing appear virtuous and anger feel inappropriate or excessive.

Parentification, Self-Trust, and Cultural Reinforcement

Parentification teaches children to prioritize external needs at the expense of their own. Cultural reinforcement later rewards this same orientation. Together, they create a powerful loop: early responsibility erodes self-trust, and cultural validation discourages its recovery.

When anger arises, it is filtered through guilt, self-questioning, and concern for others 'comfort. The individual learns to mistrust internal cues, assuming that discomfort reflects personal inadequacy rather than a meaningful signal.

Over time, the loss of self-trust becomes the most damaging consequence of guilt-absorbing anger. Without access to reliable internal signals, decisions feel uncertain, boundaries feel risky, and anger feels illegitimate—even when it is warranted.

Understanding this interplay helps reframe the problem. What appears as passivity or over-responsibility is often the residue of early adaptation reinforced by later expectation.

Toward Change

Change begins not with confrontation, but with recognition. For those who have absorbed anger for much of their lives, the first task is learning to notice anger without immediately translating it into guilt. This requires slowing down. Paying attention to bodily signals. Allowing discomfort to exist without explanation or apology. Anger, in this context, is not a call to act— but a signal to listen.

Rebuilding self-trust is a gradual process. It involves practicing small acts of self-definition: naming preferences, expressing limits, tolerating disagreement. Each act challenges the belief that connection depends on self-erasure.

Anger does not need to be eliminated to heal. It needs to be integrated—recognized as information rather than danger.

Closing Reflection

Guilt-absorbing anger is not the absence of anger, but the cost of carrying it alone. When anger is finally allowed into awareness—without blame or urgency—it no longer needs to turn inward.

What emerges is not aggression, but clarity.

Not rupture, but self-trust.

Not abandonment of others, but a return to oneself.

CHAPTER EIGHT

WHAT ARE YOU LOOKING AT?

Life Stance Anger

I stretched, got a drink of water, and walked down the hall to the waiting room to introduce myself to a new client. I had never spoken with Don before. He had been referred by a company that provided employee counseling. The session had been set up through a secretary, so I did not know what to expect.

As I entered the waiting room he abruptly stood up, held out his hand, and said, "Hi, Doc. The name is Don." He spoke with a booming, deep voice that seemed in contrast to this small, compact man. The most obvious thing about Don was the way he seemed to look right through me the first time we made eye contact. I invited him to my office. As we walked down the hall, I noticed that the logo on his tee-shirt was a skull and crossbones design.

He took a chair directly across from mine and before I could begin, he took control. In the same loud voice he said, "I figure the company is paying me for this so my plan was to stretch it out for an all day thing. But now that I see those degrees of yours I don't think that's such a good plan. I mean, what kind of a person has art if you can't tell what the hell it is?"

I began to wonder about the company that made this referral.

As Don began to describe the events that led to his referral, it became clear that his anger was not tied to a single incident. Rather, it colored nearly every interaction he described.

"They're always on my back," he said. "Supervisors, coworkers—it doesn't matter. Somebody's always trying to tell me how to do my job."

"What happens when that occurs?" I asked.

"I shut it down," he replied. "I let them know right away I'm not someone to mess with."

Don explained that he had recently been written up for intimidating behavior at work. A coworker had complained that Don's tone and posture made him feel threatened during a routine discussion. Don dismissed the complaint.

"I didn't threaten anyone," he said. "I just told him the truth. People can't handle honesty anymore."

People who interact with individuals like Don often sense the tension immediately. Before any disagreement occurs, the atmosphere is already charged. Conversations feel less like exchanges and more like confrontations waiting to happen. Over time coworkers withdraw, speak cautiously, or avoid interaction altogether—responses that unintentionally reinforce the individual's belief that others are weak, dishonest, or untrustworthy.

This tendency to come across as hostile during first encounters is typical for individuals whose life stance is organized around anger. Life stance refers to the way we view ourselves in the world—our underlying assumptions about who we are and how others are likely to treat us. If asked to describe ourselves, we typically choose adjectives such as good, caring, competent, family-oriented, indifferent, or cautious. A useful exercise for individuals seeking greater self-understanding is to make a list of these personal descriptors. In relationships, sharing such lists—when done in a calm atmosphere—can open meaningful dialogue.

Although we all attempt to see ourselves objectively, others often experience us quite differently. Those consumed with anger typically do not see themselves as clearly as those around them. Their belief is that their anger is justified and caused by the actions of others. This distorted thinking reinforces a life stance in which the world feels adversarial and threatening. To loosen anger's grip, this orientation must be examined and redefined.

In Don's mind, anger was synonymous with strength. Backing down felt like weakness. Cooperation felt like submission. His default posture—verbal, physical, and emotional—was defensive readiness. This constant readiness did not arise from momentary frustration. It reflected a broader stance toward the world: expect conflict, prepare for attack, assert dominance early.

For individuals like Don, anger is not merely an emotion or reaction. It becomes a stance toward life—a way of interpreting events, relationships, and even neutral situations through a lens of threat and opposition.

Unlike episodic anger, which rises and falls in response to circumstances, life-stance anger is constant. It organizes perception. It shapes expectations. It determines how power, safety, and vulnerability are understood.

In this pattern, anger provides structure. It creates certainty in a world experienced as unpredictable and potentially dangerous. Beneath the surface is not simply hostility, but vigilance—a continual readiness to detect and respond to threat.

Anger as Worldview

For individuals whose life stance is organized around anger, the world is perceived as inherently adversarial. Neutral actions are interpreted as challenges. Ambiguity is read as threat. The benefit of this stance is clarity—everything fits into a familiar narrative. The cost is chronic tension and isolation.

Anger becomes the organizing principle through which experience is filtered. Rather than responding to events as they arise, the individual anticipates hostility and acts preemptively. This anticipation reinforces the belief that anger is necessary for survival. Trust feels naïve. Cooperation feels dangerous. Over time, this stance becomes self-confirming. Others react defensively or withdraw, which appears to validate the original assumption: people cannot be trusted. Opportunities for cooperation diminish, and the individual feels increasingly alone, misunderstood, and justified.

Control as Protection Against Uncertainty

For individuals whose life stance is organized around anger, control often functions as a defense against uncertainty and vulnerability.

Anger narrows the field of experience. It simplifies complex interactions into clear categories of right and wrong, strong and weak, safe and unsafe. In this way, control becomes a way to reduce ambiguity and regain a sense of predictability.

Uncertainty requires tolerance—of not knowing, of waiting, of being affected by others. Vulnerability requires openness to disappointment, rejection, or misunderstanding. For those shaped by early environments where unpredictability carried real emotional cost, these states can feel intolerable.

Anger offers an alternative. It asserts dominance, sets limits quickly, and minimizes exposure. Over time, control becomes mistaken for safety. The individual may feel calmer only when situations are tightly managed and others are kept at emotional distance. Yet this control comes at a price. Relationships lose flexibility, curiosity diminishes, and genuine connection is sacrificed for certainty. Seen in this light, the life stance anger pattern is not simply about hostility—it is about managing fear through forceful clarity.

The Reinforcement Loop

The life stance anger pattern is reinforced by short-term outcomes. Anger often succeeds in stopping others, ending conversations, or asserting control. These immediate effects feel empowering and reinforce the behavior. What remains unseen are the cumulative losses: strained relationships, missed opportunities, and a narrowing of emotional range. Because anger "works" in the moment, its long-term cost is easily discounted.

As this loop continues, anger gradually shifts from response to identity. It becomes the lens through which self-worth is measured and safety is maintained.

Early Formation of a Hostile Worldview

Early experiences often reinforce the idea that vulnerability invites harm. This orientation rarely develops in a vacuum. It often emerges from environments characterized by instability, neglect, harsh discipline, or chronic unpredictability. Children in such settings learn quickly that safety cannot be assumed. Caregivers may have been inconsistent, authoritarian, or dismissive. Emotional expression may have been met with ridicule or punishment. In these environments, children learn to rely on strength rather than openness. Sensitivity becomes dangerous. Curiosity becomes risky. Anger, by contrast, offers clarity and protection.

Over time, this stance solidifies. The child stops asking whether the world is safe and instead assumes it is not. Interactions are approached as contests rather than exchanges. Control becomes the primary means of regulation. Many individuals who develop a life stance organized around anger have limited experience with reciprocity—the back-and-forth exchange in which influence is mutual and power is shared. Early relationships may have been defined by dominance, submission, or unpredictability rather than negotiation and repair.

As adults, these individuals often gravitate toward environments that reduce relational ambiguity and clearly define authority. Highly structured systems with explicit hierarchies can feel stabilizing, offering clarity where reciprocity once felt unsafe or confusing.

Attachment and the Expectation of Threat

From an attachment perspective, the life stance organized around anger is often associated with early relational experiences in which caregivers were unpredictable, rejecting, or intermittently punitive. In these environments, children learn that closeness does not reliably bring comfort and that openness may invite humiliation, control, or harm. Over time an internal expectation forms: people are not to be trusted. Dependence feels unsafe. Vigilance becomes necessary.

Anger, in this context, functions as both boundary and shield—keeping others at a distance while preserving a sense of autonomy and control. What appears later as hostility is often the residue of an early attachment lesson: connection requires defense.

Reinforcement Beyond the Family

As individuals move into adulthood, this anger-based life stance is often reinforced by broader cultural messages. Media representations of masculinity, feminine power, and success frequently equate dominance with competence and aggression with confidence.

In workplaces, assertiveness may be rewarded without regard for its impact. In social settings, intimidation can be mistaken for leadership. These reinforcements strengthen the belief that anger is not only necessary, but effective.

For someone like Don, each instance of compliance or withdrawal by others confirmed his worldview. Anger worked. Control felt justified.

Arnold

If Don represents the life-stance anger pattern in everyday conflict, Arnold illustrates what this stance can look like when it becomes deeply embedded within a family system.

Arnold arrived for therapy accompanied by his wife, though it quickly became clear that he did not view himself as the one with a problem. He sat rigidly upright, jaw set, speaking only when addressed directly and doing so with an unmistakable air of authority.

His wife, by contrast, appeared anxious and deferential, glancing toward him before answering even simple questions, as if gauging whether her response would be acceptable.

When asked what had brought them in, she began cautiously, describing tension at home, frequent arguments, and her growing fear of his temper. Arnold listened without interrupting, his expression tightening with each sentence.

Finally he spoke.

"She exaggerates," he said flatly. "I don't have a temper. I just expect things to be done right."

His tone was not loud, but it carried an unmistakable threat—not of immediate violence, but of consequences. Control, not volatility, defined his presence.

As the session continued, a pattern emerged. Arnold monitored everything: how money was spent, how the house was maintained, where his wife went, who she spoke with, and how the children behaved. Deviations from his expectations were met with criticism, withdrawal, or escalating hostility.

He described this not as control, but as responsibility.

"If I don't keep things in line," he said, "everything falls apart."

Arnold's worldview was built on the conviction that order must be enforced. He equated leadership with dominance and interpreted disagreement as disrespect.

His childhood provided important context. He grew up in a home marked by instability and unpredictability. His father was harsh and authoritarian, his mother withdrawn and unable to intervene effectively. Mistakes were punished severely. Praise was rare. Safety depended on compliance.

Arnold learned early that the only reliable protection was strength. Showing fear invited attack. Seeking comfort led to disappointment. Over time he internalized a simple rule:

Control yourself, control others, or be controlled.

As an adult, this translated into relentless vigilance. Trust required tolerance for uncertainty—the willingness to believe that others will act in good faith without constant monitoring. For Arnold, this felt intolerable. Instead, he substituted surveillance and correction for connection.

His wife described feeling as though she lived under inspection. Even small decisions required justification. Over time she stopped expressing preferences altogether, believing it was easier to comply than to endure confrontation. Ironically, the more she withdrew, the more Arnold tightened control, interpreting her silence as irresponsibility or deception.

The Cost of a Hardened Stance

Although an anger-based life stance can feel protective, its costs accumulate quietly over time. Relationships narrow. Curiosity diminishes. Opportunities for collaboration or intimacy are filtered through suspicion.

Individuals who rely on anger as a default orientation often report feeling misunderstood or disrespected, yet also isolated. Others may comply, withdraw, or avoid conflict altogether, reinforcing the individual's belief that force is necessary. Because anger discourages vulnerability, emotional range contracts. Sadness, fear, longing, and tenderness are suppressed or converted into irritation and hostility. The individual may feel strong, but that strength is brittle. It depends on constant vigilance and control.

Over time, this stance becomes exhausting.

Toward Change

Change for those whose life stance is organized around anger does not come from suppressing anger or relinquishing strength. It comes from learning to tolerate uncertainty without immediately converting it into control. This work begins with awareness—recognizing when anger is being used to eliminate discomfort rather than address a genuine threat. Pausing before reacting creates space for internal regulation. Gradually new capacities develop: the ability to stay present without dominating, the ability to disagree without attacking, and the ability to allow others their responses without interpreting them as danger. Letting go of control does not mean becoming passive. It means differentiating strength from force and safety from dominance. Over time anger no longer needs to serve as a constant shield. It returns to its proper role as a signal rather than a stance.

Closing Reflection

When anger becomes a way of life, it promises protection but delivers isolation. Releasing this stance requires courage—the courage to remain present in uncertainty and to risk vulnerability without armor. As individuals learn that connection does not always require control, the world becomes less adversarial and more open. Strength is no longer measured by readiness for battle, but by the capacity to stay engaged without force.

The patterns described in this chapter show how anger can become woven into the way individuals see the world. But anger rarely remains a private stance for long. It becomes most visible—and most complicated—when two people attempt to build a life together. In close relationships, anger patterns do not simply appear; they interact, reinforce one another, and sometimes escalate in ways neither partner fully understands.

CHAPTER NINE

IN PARTNERSHIP WITH ANGER

Anger does not only shape the person who expresses it. When it is a pattern, it also shapes the people living beside it. Not everyone expresses anger directly. Some live in its shadows—accommodating, managing, or absorbing its impact. Being constantly rehearsed, this role can become so central that the partner's own needs, perceptions, and identity begin to recede into the background.

This chapter explores the experience of those who organize their lives around another person's anger. This behavior is often misread as weakness or dependency. In reality, it represents a complex attempt to preserve connection, safety, or stability in an environment shaped by volatility. Once anger begins shaping a relationship, it doesn't remain a singular experience. It becomes the hidden partner.

How Anger Organizes a Relationship

When anger becomes a hidden partner in a relationship, it begins to organize the interaction between two people. One partner escalates, pressures, criticizes, or withdraws; the other adapts, manages, or absorbs the emotional impact. Without anyone consciously deciding it, the relationship gradually organizes itself around the management of anger.

What started as an emotional reaction slowly becomes a relational structure. The angry partner may appear to dominate the emotional climate, but the system is sustained by both people's adaptations. One expresses anger; the other learns how to live beside it.

Understanding this system is the first step toward recognizing how accommodation develops and why it can be so difficult to change.

The Cost of Accommodation

Accommodation begins as adaptation. A partner learns what triggers conflict and what reduces it. They adjust tone, timing, and expectations. They may take on additional responsibilities, anticipate reactions, or avoid topics entirely. In the short term, this strategy can reduce overt conflict. However, it often produces exhaustion, resentment, and a shrinking sense of self.

The following vignette illustrates how accommodation can become embedded in daily life.

Anne & Tanya

Anne and Tanya came to therapy together, though it was clear from the first session that Anne was the one who had insisted on it. Tanya sat back on the couch with her arms crossed, expression guarded, watching both Anne and me with open skepticism.

"I don't really see the point," Tanya said. "Nothing's going to change."

Anne's face tightened immediately.

"See? This is what I deal with," she said, turning toward me. "She just shuts down."

Tanya exhaled sharply and looked away.

Anne described their relationship as "walking on eggshells." Tanya had a temper that could flare suddenly and intensely, followed by long periods of silence or withdrawal. During those silent stretches, Anne felt responsible for repairing the connection, even when she was unsure what she had done wrong.

"I can't stand the distance," Anne said quietly. "I'll do anything to make it stop."

Tanya did not dispute this.

"She apologizes for everything," Tanya said. "Even when it's not her fault."

Anne nodded, as if this were self-evident.

"If I don't, things just get worse," she said.

As the session unfolded, a familiar pattern emerged. When tension rose, Tanya became louder, more forceful, and increasingly certain that she was being misunderstood or disrespected. Anne responded by softening her voice, conceding points she did not agree with, and shifting quickly into reassurance.

"I'm not trying to upset you," Anne said at one point. "I just want us to be okay."

Tanya's anger seemed to require a response, and Anne provided one: accommodation.

When I asked Anne what she felt in those moments, she hesitated.

"Scared," she said finally. "Not of her hurting me... just of losing her."

Tanya glanced at her, expression briefly softened, then hardened again.

"I wouldn't leave," she said. "I just need her to listen."

But listening, in practice, meant agreeing.

Anne described monitoring Tanya constantly—tone of voice, facial expression, the speed of her movements—searching for early signs of escalation. If she detected them, she adjusted herself immediately.

"I try to keep things calm," she said. "If I stay patient, it doesn't spiral."

This vigilance was exhausting, but it also gave Anne a sense of control. As long as she managed her own reactions carefully enough, she believed she could prevent Tanya's anger from becoming overwhelming.

Tanya, for her part, experienced Anne's accommodation as both comforting and irritating.

"She never just says what she really thinks," Tanya said. "It's like talking to a mirror."

Underneath the conflict was a paradox: Anne's efforts to preserve the relationship were also eroding authenticity within it.

When I asked Anne what she wanted, independent of Tanya's reactions, she looked genuinely uncertain.

"I don't know," she said slowly. "I just want us to be okay."

Her sense of self had become organized around maintaining the relationship, even at personal cost. Anne's experience highlights a central paradox: accommodation may preserve the relationship in the moment while quietly eroding it over time. The partner who accommodates becomes increasingly invisible, while the anger that drives the adaptation remains unchanged.

Anne's story illustrates how accommodation develops within the moment-to-moment dynamics of a relationship. Over time, however, this pattern does more than manage conflict—it begins to reshape the inner life of the partner who is adapting.

Why It Is Hard to Leave

From the outside, observers often ask why someone stays in a relationship marked by recurring anger. The question assumes that leaving is primarily a matter of will. In reality, multiple psychological forces make departure difficult.

There may be love, shared history, financial entanglement, children, or fear of retaliation. Just as powerful are internal forces—hope that things will improve, responsibility for the partner's well-being, or uncertainty about one's ability to function independently.

Janelle's story illustrates how these forces can accumulate over time.

Janelle

Janelle came to therapy alone, though much of her session was devoted to describing her partner's anger. She spoke quickly, as if trying to present a coherent account before her resolve faltered.

"He's not a bad person," she said repeatedly. "He just has a lot of stress."

Janelle described frequent arguments that escalated rapidly. Her partner's voice would rise, accusations would surface, and past grievances would be pulled into the present. Janelle's strategy was to de-escalate.

"I try not to react," she said. "If I stay calm, it burns out faster."

Calm, however, did not mean unaffected. Janelle reported headaches, insomnia, and a persistent sense of dread before difficult conversations.

"I can feel it building," she said. "Like pressure in the room."

When conflict erupted, she focused on soothing him rather than expressing her own feelings.

"I'll say whatever I have to," she admitted quietly. "Just to get back to normal."

Afterward, she often felt hollow, as if something essential had been pushed aside.

"I don't even remember what I was upset about," she said. "It doesn't seem important anymore."

The days accumulate and Janelle's world had narrowed. She avoided topics that might trigger arguments. She declined invitations that might provoke jealousy or resentment. Decisions were filtered through one question: How will he react?

Despite this, she remained deeply invested in the relationship.

"When things are good, they're really good," she said. "It feels worth it."

She described moments of warmth and closeness that seemed to erase the previous conflict, reinforcing her hope that stability was possible if she just handled things correctly.

When I asked what she feared most, Janelle did not hesitate.

"That he'll leave," she said. "Or that I'll push him away."

Her accommodation functioned as both protection and constraint. It minimized immediate conflict but required continual self-suppression. Janelle did not describe herself as resentful. Instead, she expressed confusion.

"I don't know when it stopped being equal," she said. "I don't know how we got here."

Her question hung in the room, less a request for explanation than a recognition that something fundamental had shifted—quietly, gradually, and without clear boundaries.

Janelle's situation reflects how accommodation can shift from a conscious choice to an entrenched pattern. What begins as flexibility gradually becomes obligation, reinforced by beliefs about loyalty, responsibility, and self-worth. Her experience shows how accommodation gradually becomes structured and embedded in the relationship.

Common Myths Partners Hold

Partners who accommodate anger often carry assumptions that sustain the pattern:

- "If I'm patient enough, things will settle."
- "If I don't provoke, there won't be conflict."
- "It's my responsibility to keep the peace."
- "Leaving would be selfish or harmful."

These beliefs can coexist with mounting distress, creating a cycle in which the partner sacrifices more while receiving less stability in return.

When Love Is Not Enough Without Boundaries

Accommodation does not always develop solely within the couple. Sometimes anger enters the relationship through outside pressures—family expectations, guilt, or manipulation—that partners struggle to resist.

Steve and Sandy had been married for 15 years. Both held steady jobs and were quick to explain that they were deeply in love with each other. Steve was 35 and Sandy was 34, having met and married while attending a local junior college. There were no children in the marriage. They seemed to have a mutual respect and were an attractive couple who shared common goals. It sounded like an Ozzie-and-Harriet type relationship.

I asked them why they had decided to seek therapy. At once Sandy began to fight back tears, and Steve transformed into a sad, visibly shaken man. Steve stated that their respective parents had been placing a lot of pressure on them to have children. It had gotten so bad recently that both Sandy's and Steve's mothers met with Sandy for lunch to confront her with "their" problem. Sandy had become extremely guilt-ridden and depressed and had not been answering the phone or attending any of the social functions to which they had recently been invited.

At virtually the same time, Steve's and Sandy's fathers had spoken with Steve, explaining how upset their wives were and wondering what Steve was going to do about it. Steve's response was that he would talk it over with Sandy and come up with a solution that would make their parents proud. In reality, he too became depressed, lost weight, wasn't sleeping well, and seemed to be contracting one cold after another since the discussion.

The combined result of this external influence was affecting their job performance as well as their relationship. They desperately wanted to help each other with the dilemma but didn't seem to know what to do.

I asked them about having children.

Steve replied, "I suppose we should. Mom says we're not getting any younger. I really hadn't planned on it yet, though."

Sandy gave her side. "I'm probably going to stop taking the pill when this prescription runs out, even though I love my job and wanted to stick with it longer before we planned for a baby."

I posed the question, "Then you've made your decision?"

Steve responded, "Well, that's why we're here. You see, we really don't want kids now."

"Then, if you both feel this way, why would you have one?"

Sandy spoke up. "Because our parents want a grandchild, and we feel bad for not giving them one."

"Are either of you angry about your parents 'demands, or tactics?"

They looked at each other several seconds before Steve started. "Well, I wish they would leave us alone—but just about children."

Sandy could no longer hold back her tears and added, "Me too."

"Steve and Sandy—think carefully. Do your parents make you feel guilty about other things?"

This was the beginning of a series of intense sessions centered around guilt induction. Neither Steve nor Sandy were able initially to relate directly to the term anger or admit that they were angry at their parents. Internally they were enraged that their parents would attempt to pressure them into having children. In each of their cases, their parents had long used guilt to manipulate and control them.

Here is a case in which both Steve and Sandy had the best of relationships, yet were being torn apart by external influences. They shared a mutual respect and, therefore, reciprocity. With help, they could continue to have a long-term relationship.

The Impact on Identity

Over time, organizing one's life around another person's anger can alter self-perception. Personal preferences, goals, and even emotional responses may be suppressed or questioned.

Individuals may struggle to answer basic questions:

- What do I want?
- What do I feel?
- What would I choose if I didn't have to manage someone else's reactions?

Tony and Vera's relationship illustrates how this erosion of identity can occur even when both partners genuinely wish to improve things.

Tony & Vera

Tony and Vera came to therapy after what Vera described as "years of going in circles." They sat apart from each other, leaving a noticeable gap on the couch between them. Tony leaned forward, elbows on his knees, while Vera sat upright, hands folded tightly in her lap.

"I don't understand what she wants from me," Tony said early in the session. "Nothing I do is ever enough."

Vera did not respond immediately. When she did, her voice was measured but tense.

"I don't want more," she said. "I want consistency."

Tony exhaled loudly, as if the word itself were unreasonable.

The pattern between them became clear as they spoke. Tony's anger surfaced quickly whenever he felt criticized or cornered. His voice rose, his gestures sharpened, and his language shifted toward absolutes.

"You always do this."

"You never let anything go."

Vera's response was the opposite. She became quieter, more controlled, choosing her words carefully. She rarely interrupted, but her restraint carried its own intensity.

"I'm trying not to escalate things," she explained.

When Tony's anger peaked, Vera withdrew emotionally. She might leave the room, end the conversation, or become silent. Tony experienced this withdrawal as abandonment, which fueled further anger.

"You just shut down," he said. "How am I supposed to fix anything if you won't talk?"

Vera shook her head.

"I stop talking because nothing I say makes it better," she replied. "It just gets louder."

Both partners believed they were responding reasonably to the other's behavior. Tony saw himself as reacting to provocation. Vera saw herself as preventing escalation. The practiced result was that their roles had hardened. Tony pursued resolution through confrontation; Vera pursued safety through disengagement. Neither strategy produced the connection they wanted.

During one session, Vera described a recent incident. Tony had come home late without calling. When she asked where he had been, he responded defensively, interpreting the question as an accusation. The conversation escalated rapidly.

"I wasn't even angry," Vera said. "I just wanted to know."

Tony interjected.

"It didn't sound like that," he said. "It sounded like I was already guilty."

As the argument intensified, Vera became quiet and left the room. Tony followed, demanding that she stay and talk. She locked herself in the bedroom.

"I needed space," she said. "I didn't feel safe continuing."

Tony described the experience differently.

"It felt like she was shutting me out," he said. "Like I didn't matter."

In therapy, it became evident that both were responding to fear—Tony to the fear of rejection, Vera to the fear of escalation. Anger and withdrawal formed a loop, each reinforcing the other.

When I asked Vera what she wanted most from Tony in those moments, she paused.

"For him to calm down," she said. "So I don't have to disappear."

When I asked Tony what he wanted from Vera, his answer was immediate.

"For her to stay," he said. "So we can fix it."

Their needs were not incompatible, but their strategies were.

Vera had learned that accommodating Tony's anger prevented worse conflict, but at the cost of her own voice. Tony had learned that pushing harder was the only way to break through her silence, even though it drove her further away.

Neither felt understood. Both felt alone.

Tony and Vera demonstrate how anger and accommodation can form a self-reinforcing system. One partner escalates to feel heard; the other withdraws to feel safe. Each response intensifies the other, making change difficult without deliberate intervention.

Understanding the pattern is the first step. The more difficult task is learning how partners can respond differently once anger begins to escalate.

Expanding Regulation in Relationship

Regulation in the presence of anger is not simply about staying calm. It involves communicating in a way that neither escalates conflict nor abandons oneself.

Partners who shift out of accommodation often discover that new responses are required, not just new boundaries.

Speaking gently does not mean agreeing. It means refusing to match escalation with escalation. Showing interest does not mean surrendering one's position. It means demonstrating that the relationship still matters even during disagreement. Validation does not require endorsing the other person's behavior; it acknowledges the reality of their emotional experience. An easy, non-defensive manner can prevent conflict from hardening into battle.

These behaviors create space for dialogue rather than dominance. They allow anger to be expressed without turning the interaction into a contest of power. Importantly, such responses are most effective when paired with clear limits. Without boundaries, gentleness becomes accommodation. Without empathy, boundaries become rejection. Regulation lives in the space where firmness and care coexist.

Regulation in Real Time: Tony & Vera

Tony and Vera's conflict did not persist because either of them lacked insight. Both understood, at least intellectually, what was happening. What they lacked was a way to stay present with one another once anger entered the room.

Tony tended to escalate when he felt ignored or disrespected. Vera withdrew when she felt overwhelmed or criticized. Each reaction intensified the other.

Change began not with dramatic confrontation, but with learning how to respond differently in small moments.

For Tony, this meant lowering intensity without abandoning his point. Instead of raising his voice or repeating himself more forcefully, he learned to speak more slowly and directly: "I'm upset and I want to be heard, not to fight."

For Vera, regulation meant staying present rather than disappearing. Withdrawal had protected her for years, but it also left Tony feeling alone and unheard.

Both partners learned to acknowledge the other's emotional reality without surrendering their own perspective. These changes may sound small, but their impact was profound. Conflict slowed. Escalation became less automatic. Each partner felt less alone and less threatened.

Through trial and error, successes and missteps, Tony discovered that he did not need to dominate to be heard. Vera discovered that she did not need to disappear to stay safe.

Toward Change

Change rarely occurs through insight alone. It requires practicing new behaviors while tolerating the discomfort they produce.

For the accommodating partner this may include:

- Expressing needs directly
- Allowing the other person to experience consequences
- Resisting the urge to smooth over conflict
- Building independent sources of support
- Reconnecting with personal values and goals

For the partner prone to anger, change involves developing regulation skills, tolerating frustration, and learning non-coercive ways of engaging. Sustainable improvement depends on both individuals having the motivation and willingness to participate in the hard work of change and growth.

Closing Reflection

Living in partnership with anger often means carrying more than one's share of emotional responsibility. The relentlessness of this burden can obscure the possibility of a different way of relating. Many partners slowly organize themselves around maintaining peace. Preferences narrow. Self-expression becomes cautious. What is lost is not only comfort, but visibility.

Reclaiming oneself within a relationship does not require abandoning love. It requires relinquishing the belief that love must be purchased through self-erasure. Healthy relationships are not defined by the absence of anger. They are defined by the ability to remain visible to one another when anger appears.

Love that requires disappearance cannot sustain intimacy. Love that allows both people to remain visible—even when upset, imperfect, or uncertain—creates the conditions for genuine safety.

CHAPTER TEN

THE CURATIVE PATH

Elevating Understanding: Awareness & Orientation

Lasting change rarely begins with force of will. It begins with clarity. Many people arrive at this point after years of reacting in ways they do not fully understand—feeling unconsciously driven rather than consciously choosing, trapped rather than free. The curative path begins when anger is no longer experienced as something that simply "happens," but as a pattern that can be observed, understood, and gradually reshaped. Awareness is the first on-ramp to the curative path because it transforms anger from an unquestioned reflex into something that can be observed, understood, and eventually reshaped.

Anger patterns do not emerge in isolation. They are shaped by experience, reinforced over time, and often maintained because they once served an important function. Recognizing this does not excuse harmful behavior, but it does replace shame with understanding. What made sense in one context may no longer serve in another.

Orientation also involves recognizing that change will not occur in a single dramatic shift. The nervous system tends to return to familiar pathways, especially under stress. Habits of thought and expectations within relationships often reinforce these same patterns. Awareness creates the space in which a different response becomes possible, even if only briefly at first. From this perspective, setbacks are not failures but information. Each reaction reveals where capacity is strong and where it remains fragile. Over time, repeated moments of noticing—before, during, or after anger—gradually weaken the automatic nature of the response.

Embodied Responsibility: Regulation & Ownership

Insight alone rarely produces change. Without regulation, awareness can even intensify distress by making patterns visible without providing the capacity to alter them. Responsibility in this context means developing the ability to manage internal states rather than attempting to control external circumstances or other people.

Regulation is both capacity and skill. It involves learning to tolerate emotional activation without immediate discharge, suppression, or escape. This may include pausing, tracking bodily sensations, grounding attention, or engaging in physical movement that dissipates arousal without fueling aggression. In practical terms, regulation often begins with very small actions. Slowing the pace of breathing, pausing before responding, stepping briefly away from an escalating exchange, or simply naming what one is feeling can interrupt the automatic cycle of anger. These actions may seem minor, yet they shift the nervous system from reaction toward reflection. Over time, such interruptions accumulate, gradually weakening the reflexive pull of anger and strengthening the capacity for deliberate choice. As regulation improves, choice emerges.

What once felt inevitable becomes optional. The individual can remain present long enough to consider consequences, alternatives, and values.

Many people find it helpful to cultivate an observing stance—sometimes called the "witness." From this position, emotions are experienced without being mistaken for identity. One can notice anger rising, peaking, and subsiding rather than becoming engulfed by it. This does not eliminate intensity, but it changes the relationship to it. Ownership follows naturally. Responsibility shifts from blaming circumstances or other people toward acknowledging one's own role in responses. Importantly, ownership is not self-condemnation. It is the recognition that change lies within one's sphere of influence.

Integration and Reconnection: Returning to the True Self

As anger loses its central organizing role, something unexpected often emerges: unfamiliar emotional territory. Without the intensity, certainty, or protective function of anger, many encounter grief, vulnerability, loneliness, or uncertainty that had previously been masked. A discovery that beneath the anger language they relied on for years—whether retaliatory, guilt-inducing, withdrawn, or explosive—were emotions that had never been fully experienced or expressed. When anger begins to loosen its hold, these previously hidden feelings often emerge with surprising intensity. The curative path therefore does not eliminate emotion; it expands the emotional vocabulary available to a person.

Integration involves welcoming these experiences rather than interpreting them as weakness. It also involves rediscovering aspects of the self that were suppressed in order to survive earlier conditions—curiosity, playfulness, tenderness, creativity, or the capacity for closeness. This process can feel disorienting. The familiar identity organized around anger is giving way to something less rigid and less predictable. Some people describe it as learning to inhabit their own lives for the first time.

Reconnection to the "true self" does not mean returning to a pre-injury state; it means building a coherent identity that includes both strength and vulnerability. Emotional range expands. Relationships become less adversarial and more reciprocal. Decisions are guided less by fear and more by values.

Writing as a Tool for Change

A journal or diary is a useful way to begin identifying patterns—especially those times when you respond to situations with anger. While you may ultimately aim to replace anger with other responses, this is a gradual process and setbacks are to be expected. Writing helps clarify patterns and makes visible the particular ways anger has functioned in your life. After an angry reaction, record what happened and consider how the situation might have been handled differently. Experiment on paper with alternative responses and emotions. With consistent repetition, this process can reveal new options that may later become available in real situations.

Try putting these alternatives into practice and then write about the experience again:

- Did it work?
- How did it feel to be direct without becoming angry?
- Were you sincere in your effort?
- What made it easier or harder?

Maintaining an ongoing record of your progress is an important part of this technique. Periodically review earlier entries to see how far you have come.

If you are in a relationship with another person who struggles with anger, sharing selected journal entries—when it feels safe—can help both of you recognize progress as well as recurring difficulties. When anger arises, writing down the cause and your emotional state can itself reduce the intensity of the reaction. For some individuals, the brief pause required to put feelings into words is enough to prevent an impulsive angry response.

Even if journaling feels difficult at first, it can become a powerful tool for increasing self-knowledge and supporting change.

Support Network

Developing a support network can be challenging, particularly for individuals who struggle with trust. Yet feedback from others is often essential for recognizing patterns and making meaningful change. Because anger can make relationships unpredictable, close friendships may be limited. Others may feel uncertain about when the next outburst might occur or whether they might become the target. This unpredictability can be intimidating and exhausting for those who want to remain close. Building supportive relationships therefore requires intentional effort:

- Establish and nurture connections gradually
- Practice honesty about your struggles with anger
- Accept feedback without defensiveness
- Avoid directing anger toward those who are trying to help

Supportive feedback does not always take the form of confrontation. Often it emerges through simple observations from trusted individuals: "Something about that situation seemed to escalate quickly," or "You seemed hurt before the anger appeared." Such reflections can help identify patterns that are difficult to recognize from within one's own experience. Breaking long-standing anger patterns often requires moving out of isolation. Remaining alone can reinforce resentment, hopelessness, or depression. Taking interpersonal risks—sharing honestly, staying engaged, and working to maintain relationships—creates opportunities to develop new ways of relating that are not organized around anger.

Take Steps Toward Personal Growth

As anger begins to lose its central role, it becomes possible to expand into new experiences. Taking manageable social risks can support this process. For example, enrolling in a class, pursuing a new interest, or participating in structured activities can help rebuild confidence and competence outside familiar patterns.

The following example illustrates how this broader expansion of emotional life can unfold over time.

Jack—Recovery and Emotional Expansion

Jack sought counseling at age 31 after his wife left because of his out-of-control behavior. For months he projected blame outward and could not recognize the consequences of his actions. It took nearly a year after the separation for him to reach a point where change became possible.

Treatment involved two years of weekly therapy. Early on, the therapist outlined predictable reactions Jack would likely have in treatment. This established that his behavior followed a pattern rather than being uniquely justified—and that attempts to intimidate or manipulate the process would not succeed.

During the denial phase, Jack repeatedly became angry when his worldview was not validated. He left sessions, cancelled appointments, and intensified his efforts to prove he was right. Paradoxically, this escalation indicated progress: maintaining his old pattern was requiring more effort. With consistent confrontation delivered in a supportive manner, Jack gradually accepted responsibility. Once a therapeutic alliance formed, video feedback was introduced so he could see how others experienced him. Watching himself on tape was overwhelming. He withdrew from therapy for a period—another predicted phase—before returning and engaging more deeply. Therapy then focused on childhood origins, moving in a "two steps forward, one step back" rhythm. Initially, insight triggered intense anger toward his parents. Eventually he learned that staying there did not support recovery. Later work emphasized developing alternative emotional responses. Jack practiced observing interactions without intervening angrily and learned to identify emotions beyond anger using feeling charts and role-play exercises.

Anger expression was restricted; when it surfaced, he used substitutes such as running, basketball, or journaling. With practice, he learned to replace anger with a range of appropriate emotional responses.

Now attending therapy only occasionally, Jack maintains stable relationships and a supportive network. Anxiety about long-term commitment—once impossible for him to acknowledge—became evidence of genuine emotional engagement.

He summarized his progress simply:

"I know I'm getting better because I can feel sad, I can laugh—even laugh at myself—and I can listen to myself and trust my feelings."

Recovery did not eliminate conflict or stress. It restored emotional range and coping capacity.

Jason—Aftermath of Early Patterns

Jason, first introduced earlier in the book, experienced severe difficulties after release from juvenile detention at age eighteen. He became involved in fights, drugs, alcohol, gambling, and repeated arrests. After a final arrest, a judge mandated therapy and participation in Alcoholics Anonymous. The legal pressure initially motivated compliance.

Jason was referred to a therapist who implemented a behavioral re-education program similar to Jack's. He attended AA several times per week while working to reduce inappropriate anger expression.

Eighteen months later, Jason continued treatment voluntarily. He remained abstinent from substances and overt hostility, avoided arrests, and began maintaining a responsible lifestyle.

He later contacted the therapist to report progress and asked:

"I've accomplished all these good things… I'm living a responsible life now, so when do I get happy?"

This question marked a new stage: the loss of the stimulation and intensity that anger had previously provided. Without it, many individuals experience emptiness.

Jason had missed opportunities to develop close relationships, compassion toward self and others, and meaningful interests. Therapy shifted toward building those capacities rather than merely suppressing behavior. Recovery required accepting that healthy emotional life may feel quieter than the intensity of anger-driven living.

Jason's experience illustrates an important truth: recovery is not only about reducing destructive behavior but about learning how to live within a different emotional landscape.

Living the Change

Boundaries, Voice, and Ongoing Practice

Understanding anger patterns can bring relief, clarity, and even grief. Yet insight alone does not change daily life. Change becomes real through repeated moments in which a person chooses to respond differently—to speak, to pause, to set limits, to remain present, or sometimes to step away.

Many people recognize the language of "boundaries" but struggle to know what it actually means in practice. They are expressions of self-respect that clarify what one is responsible for and what one is not. They allow connection without self-erasure and autonomy without isolation.

In clinical work, it is not uncommon for individuals to admit—often with embarrassment—that while they have heard the language of "setting boundaries" repeatedly, they are unsure what it actually means in practice. Boundaries are frequently spoken of as if they are self-evident, when in fact they are skills that develop only when internal authority and regulation are in place. Boundaries are not walls, ultimatums, or attempts to control others. They are expressions of self-clarity. A boundary begins internally, with the ability to notice one's limits, values, and needs, and to take those signals seriously. Assertive rights provide the internal permission required for boundaries to exist at all. Without them, boundary-setting becomes either explosive, passive, or avoided entirely.

When anger has long functioned as the primary means of asserting oneself, boundaries often feel unfamiliar or unsafe. In this context, reclaiming assertive rights is not about becoming more forceful, but about becoming more precise. Boundaries emerge naturally when individuals can recognize what they feel, name what they need, and choose responses that honor both self and relationship.

First Experience of Boundary Awareness

~ "I used to think boundaries meant telling someone off or drawing a hard line. That never felt like me. What I began to notice instead was a tightening in my chest when I agreed to something I didn't want to do. For a long time, I ignored that feeling and told myself it wasn't a big deal. When I finally slowed down enough to stay with it, I realized the boundary wasn't something I had to announce—it was something I had to acknowledge."

~ "The first boundary I practiced wasn't spoken out loud. It was simply noticing, "I don't want this," and allowing that to matter. Later, when I did speak, it sounded smaller than I expected: "I can't do that today." No explanation. No apology. The relationship didn't end. I didn't fall apart. What changed was that I felt more solid inside myself."

At the heart of boundary-setting lies a set of fundamental personal rights. These rights are not privileges granted by others; they are inherent aspects of psychological health. For those who grew up in environments where needs were minimized, punished, or ignored, these rights may feel unfamiliar or even uncomfortable. Reclaiming them is part of the curative path.

A First Step Toward Boundaries

One person described her first attempt at setting a boundary this way:

"I thought boundaries meant confrontation or rejection. It never occurred to me that I could simply state what I needed. The first time I said, 'I can't do that tonight, but I can help tomorrow, ' I waited for something terrible to happen—anger, withdrawal, punishment. None of that happened. It was awkward, but it was also freeing. I realized I didn't have to disappear to keep the peace."

Often, the first step is not dramatic. It is a small, clear statement of preference or limit, delivered without apology or aggression. Each such moment strengthens self-trust and demonstrates that connection can survive honesty.

Ten Assertive Rights

You have the right:

To be treated with respect.

To express your feelings, opinions, and needs honestly.

To say no without guilt or excessive justification.

To make mistakes and learn from them.

To change your mind.

To prioritize your physical and emotional well-being.

To ask for what you want, recognizing that others may decline.

To set limits on what you will tolerate.

To choose how you spend your time, energy, and attention.

To pursue a life that reflects your values rather than others ' expectations.

These rights do not negate responsibility for the impact of one's behavior. Rather, they create the foundation from which responsible and authentic interaction becomes possible.

For many people, simply reading these statements evokes a mixture of relief and discomfort. Both reactions are understandable. Relief reflects recognition; discomfort reflects how unfamiliar these permissions may be.

Questions for Ongoing Reflection

The following questions are not a test. They are intended to help you observe how anger has functioned in your life and where change may be occurring.

Consider them periodically, especially during times of transition:

When I feel anger rising, can I notice it before acting on it?

Do I recognize the needs or vulnerabilities beneath my anger?

Am I able to express concerns directly rather than indirectly or explosively?

Do I allow others to have perspectives different from my own without needing to win?

Am I building relationships that support growth rather than reinforce old patterns?

In difficult moments, do I respond in ways that align with my values rather than my impulses?

Your answers may shift over time. You can track this through incorporating this into your journaling practice. In so doing, you will note that progress is rarely linear and be able to see that periods of regression often precede new levels of stability.

Change as a Continuing Practice

Living differently does not mean eliminating anger or conflict. It means developing the capacity to experience strong emotion without being defined by it. Each moment of awareness, regulation, honesty, or restraint strengthens new neural and relational pathways. Some days will feel easier than others. Stress, loss, illness, or major life transitions can temporarily reactivate old patterns. These moments do not erase progress; they simply indicate areas that require renewed attention and care.

Support from others—friends, partners, mentors, or therapists—can help sustain change. Equally important is the development of an internal stance of compassion toward oneself. Harsh self-criticism often fuels the very reactions one hopes to change.

Throughout this book we have explored different anger languages—the habitual ways individuals translate distress, fear, disappointment, or vulnerability into anger. The curative path does not silence emotion; it teaches a new translation. As emotional awareness grows, anger becomes only one possible response rather than the dominant language through which experience is expressed.

A Final Thought

At the beginning of this exploration, anger may have appeared chaotic, destructive, or impossible to control—something that simply erupted leaving consequences in its wake. Yet anger rarely emerges without meaning. It develops within relationships, experiences, and attempts to cope with emotional pain. When its language is understood, it no longer needs to dominate the emotional landscape. It becomes one signal among many—informative, but no longer in command.

Anger once served a purpose. It protected, energized, or signaled distress when other options were unavailable. Honoring that history allows the past to be integrated rather than denied.

The curative path is not about becoming someone entirely new. It is about becoming more fully oneself—capable of strength without aggression, vulnerability without collapse, and connection without self-loss.

Change is less a destination than a direction. Each step toward awareness, responsibility, and authenticity reshapes the landscape of one's life.

You do not have to walk this path perfectly. You only have to keep walking.

CLOSING NOTE

When the original work that gave rise to this book was written, I was in the midst of building both a professional life and an understanding of the human experience that felt urgent and immediate. Now, at seventy—twice the age I was then—I see those early efforts with both appreciation and perspective. Much has changed in the field, in the culture, and in my own life. What has remained constant is the recognition that growth is not a single achievement but an ongoing process of adaptation.

The principles described in these pages have not existed only in my work with others; they have been present in my own life as well. Like anyone else, I have encountered loss, uncertainty, missteps, and the need to revise long-held assumptions. The pursuit of knowledge has been less about accumulating answers than about remaining flexible enough to ask better questions over time.

Much of my greatest satisfaction has come from continuing to engage in the therapeutic process. To sit with another person as they explore their inner world—to witness courage, resistance, grief, humor, and resilience—is both a responsibility and a privilege. The individuals who have entrusted me with their stories have taught me as much as any formal training. Their willingness to confront painful truths and to keep moving forward has been a constant source of inspiration.

If this book offers anything of value, it is not a formula for change but an invitation to remain open—to oneself, to others, and to the possibility that growth can occur at any stage of life. Adaptation does not end when youth fades; in many ways, it deepens.

I remain grateful for the opportunity to continue this work and for the reminder, again and again, that understanding is never final. It evolves as we do.

SELECTED READINGS

The following works informed the development of this book and may be useful to readers who wish to explore these topics further:

- Bowlby, J.—Attachment and Loss
- Brown, B.—Daring Greatly
- Damasio, A.—The Feeling of What Happens
- Fonagy, P.—Affect Regulation, Mentalization, and the Development of the Self
- Gottman, J.—The Seven Principles for Making Marriage Work
- LeDoux, J.—The Emotional Brain
- Linehan, M.—Cognitive-Behavioral Treatment of Borderline Personality Disorder
- Porges, S.—The Polyvagal Theory
- Siegel, D.—The Developing Mind
- van der Kolk, B.—The Body Keeps the Score

INDEX

W